P9-BII-602

THE ART OF POLITICAL WAR

THE ART OF POLITICAL WAR
and Other Radical Pursuits

DAVID HOROWITZ

SPENCE PUBLISHING COMPANY · DALLAS
2000

Copyright © 2000 by Americom Strategies, Inc.
First impression July 2000
Second impression September 2000

All rights reserved. No part of this publication may be reproduced or transmitted in any form or by any means, electronic or mechanical, including photocopy, recording, or any information storage and retrieval system now known or to be invented, without permission in writing from the publisher, except by a reviewer who wishes to quote brief passages in connection with a review written for inclusion in a magazine, newspaper, or broadcast.

Published in the United States by
Spence Publishing Company
111 Cole Street
Dallas, Texas 75207

Library of Congress Cataloging-in-Publication Data

Horowitz, David, 1939-
    The art of political war : and other radical pursuits / David Horowitz.
        p. cm.
    Includes bibliographical references and index.
    ISBN 1-890626-28-7
    1. Conservatism—United States.   2. Politics, Practical—United
States.   3. Right and left (Political science).   I. Title.
    JC573.2.U6 H667 2000
    324.7'2'0973—dc21   00-032988

Printed in the United States of America

To my political mentor, Michael,

to Tom Gammon and Wally Nunn,

who encouraged me,

and to my wife, April,

for her loving support of all my efforts

Contents

IV

RADICAL PURSUITS

V

LAST WORDS

A Political Sea Change

F ROM THE END OF THE CIVIL WAR until George McGovern's 1972 campaign for president, politics in America was a family affair. In contrast to Europe, where conflicts pitted socialists against conservatives and often erupted in revolution and civil war, American politics involved little or no social upheaval. Whatever divided Americans was not fundamental; elections were about nuts-and-bolts issues, not about the foundations of the republic itself.

Critics complained that the two parties were no more different than Tweedledum and Tweedledee and offered voters "an echo, not a choice." But there was also a bright side to this political convergence: it reflected the common values and shared understandings of the American social contract. Elections may have lacked ideological drama, but the payoff was political stability and the sense of a common national purpose, which seemed well worth the price.

All this changed in the 1960s with the emergence of an ideological left in the heart of America's political culture. This countercultural movement was socialist in content and radical in its approach. Its leaders styled themselves revolutionaries, turned their backs on democratic elections, and took their causes "to the streets." They rejected the political parties, calling them pawns of a "corporate ruling class." Democracy, they groused, was a "sham." But the revolutionary idea proved elusive in democratic America, and in 1972 the radicals of the 1960s abandoned the battle of the streets to join the presidential campaign of antiwar candidate George McGovern. In the aftermath of Watergate and the Nixon impeachment, they assumed a new role as the activist core of the Democratic Party.

As a result of these developments, today the Democratic Party draws its strength from the ideological left, a constituency composed of government unions, whose agenda is the expansion of governmental power, and organizations that grew out of the crusades of the 1960s and are driven by racial grievances, environmental radicalism, and campaigns for reproductive and welfare rights.

Philosophically, the Democratic Party is now almost indistinguishable from the traditional left-wing parties of Europe that make up the "Second Socialist International." The affinity of the Democrats for the socialist Labour Party in Britain is as emblematic of the change as is the Democratic National Committee's choice of Carlottia Scott—a former mistress of the Marxist dictator of Grenada and a veteran of the hard left—to be its "political issues director." Yet this 1999 appointment was so much in character for the progressive coalition that now directs the Democratic Party that the appointment did not raise a single eyebrow among the Republican opposition.

At the most basic level, Democrats now view "rights"—the key concept of democratic politics—through the same lens as the traditional left, as social entitlements that can be created by government. This is not the view of rights held by the American Founders, but the classic socialist view. It can be traced to the French, but not the American, Revolution. It is a view both parties previously understood to be at odds with the idea of liberty enshrined in the Constitution of the American Republic.

Both the Declaration of Independence and the Constitution re-gard entitlements as endowments, not of human governments, but of a divine Creator. The rights to "life, liberty, and the pursuit of happiness" are not given by the state, nor can they be taken away by political agencies—not even when those agencies represent the people itself: they are "inalienable." In the eyes of the Founders, govern-ment is instituted only to secure the rights that God has given. The state cannot create additional entitlements as it would new taxes. Government-conferred "rights" are therefore negative in nature. They establish limits to what government may do. That is why the Bill of Rights is framed in negatives: "Congress shall make no law. . . ."*

This common understanding of the Constitution as setting lim-its to what government may do has now broken down. (This is the second such national breakdown, the first having led to the Civil War.) This breakdown is usually referred to as a "culture war" and is the direct consequence of the entry of the left into the American mainstream. Leftists view the Constitution as a "living" document, and hence a malleable instrument of their "progressive" policies and socialist schemes the Founders would have found anathema. As a result of the influence of these views, the manufacture of rights has become a cottage industry of Democratic legislators and the judges they appoint, and a principal battleground of the culture war. The left's ambition in these battles is to circumvent the checks and bal-ances that were erected by the Framers to thwart what Madison de-scribed as the "wicked projects" of social levelers.† The core agenda of the left (which includes its tax formulas, its racial preferences, and

---

* The classic discussion of these differing views of rights is Isaiah Berlin's *Two Concepts of Liberty*.

† *The Federalist*, Number 10. See my discussion of this conflict in *The Politics of Bad Faith* (New York: Free Press, 2000), 147ff, 185.

its welfare claims) is to redistribute individual income on the basis of political prejudice. This is the essential socialist idea. The "culture war" that has defined "conservatives" and "liberals" for the past quarter of a century is in many ways just another name for the ideological conflicts between socialists and conservatives familiar from the European past.

Of course, the past never simply repeats itself. The influence of radicals inside the Democratic Party does not mean that the Democratic Party itself is a radical organization or that America is necessarily on the brink of social upheaval. Indeed, it would be odd if that were the case. The world left has suffered grievous defeats in the collapse of its utopian schemes over the last century. Its radical temper has been severely chastened by the historic collapse of Communism and the failure of socialist plans. Defeats of such magnitude have not caused the left to give up its long-range agendas, but they have made the left more pragmatic in attempting to achieve them.

Contemporary leftists (often misidentified as "liberals"*) are less impatient than they once were to pursue a radical course. The term "piecemeal revolution" would more aptly describe their current efforts. If the American people shut the front door on socialized medicine, for example, leftists will try to bring it in by the back door. They understand how to tack against the political winds and are able, during election cycles, to make temporary peace with balanced budgets and welfare reforms while they replot their political course. They are willing to compromise, work in coalitions, and be practical about what they can accomplish. Philosophically, they speculate about a "Third Way" between socialism and capitalism, which has long been a traditional escape route from the cul de sac of leftist defeats. But through all their linguistic shuffles and political temporizing the social

---

* Ibid., where I discuss this distortion in our political vocabulary at length.

vision that inspires them is still the impossible dream of a humanity remade.

This is the "mend it, don't end it" school of pragmatic utopianism —or "practical idealism," as Al Gore described it. Bill Clinton's successful compromise with Republicans on balanced budgets and welfare reform rescued the Democratic Party from the electoral irrelevance to which its leftist trends had almost condemned it. But the tactical nature of this retreat has been manifest in the Democrats' continuing pressure for expansive programs and "progressive" agendas. The big government leopard has hardly changed its spots. Moreover, it is unlikely a Democratic leader will soon emerge who is philosophically to the right of William Jefferson Clinton. Barring a disastrous electoral defeat, it is even more unlikely that the party itself will undergo a change of political heart.

The title essay of this book—"The Art of Political War"—was written to address one consequence of the transformation of the Democratic Party into a party of the left. This is the challenge presented to Republicans in the way Democrats conduct the political battle. A remarkable fact of the decade following the fall of the Berlin Wall was the resurgence of the Democratic Party through its appropriation of Republican rhetoric and policy. During the 1980s and 1990s, Americans rejected liberal Democratic agendas and ratified conservative Republican policies on balanced budgets, welfare reform, crime, and family values. But it was the Democrats, at the national level, who reaped the electoral rewards. In 1996, Bill Clinton was elected for a second term by running on what was basically Newt Gingrich's Republican "Contract With America."

It is my view that these developments cannot be attributed solely to the co-opting of these policies by Bill Clinton and his strategist Dick Morris. Nor is it merely due to the self-discipline of the Democratic Party left (which regularly subordinates its radical agendas to electoral opportunity). These developments reveal that the left-wing activists who now make up the core of the Democratic Party understand the nature of political war in our democracy, and Republicans quite simply do not. "The Art of Political War" is an instructional guide to making up this deficit.

"The Art of Political War" was originally published as a pamphlet and has been endorsed by Republican National Committee Chairman Jim Nicholson, by Karl Rove, manager of the Bush presidential campaign, and by thirty-four state Republican Party chairs. Whether this portends a sea change in Republican strategy remains to be seen. Readers of the original pamphlet will find it significantly expanded here, and the text itself has been revised throughout.

The second section deals with the seduction of conservatives (who should know better) by the Puritan impulse, a powerful force in American politics, with constituencies at both ends of the political spectrum. Liberty is what conservatism is—or should be—about, not more government supervision of a "helpless" citizenry it thinks has been put in its care.

The third section addresses current controversies on race and describes my involvement in them both as a columnist for *Salon* and as the author of *Hating Whitey and Other Progressive Causes*. Much of this section is a reworking and knitting together of articles that originally appeared in *Salon.com*.

The last two sections extend this excursion into the "culture wars" and continue my efforts to deconstruct the radical mentality of the American left. All these chapters originally appeared as articles in *Salon.com*.

I WISH TO THANK my editors at *Salon.com*, David Talbot and David Weir, for providing me this unique platform in the Internet world.

Benjamin Kepple's careful copyediting and fact-checking once again made this text better and more accurate than it would otherwise have been. I want to thank John Kurzweil for being a good critic and my Dallas publisher Thomas Spence and his able executives Mitchell Muncy, Chad Blando, Yannick Ratnayake, and William Tierney for their courageous efforts to do for this and my previous book what my New York publishers would not.

I

The Art of Political War

THE REPUBLICAN PARTY claims to be the party of personal responsibility, yet it has become a party that takes no responsibility for the predicaments in which it finds itself. Instead, Republicans blame bias in the media, or the liar in the White House, or their unprincipled opponents, or even the immorality of the American people to explain their defeats.

How can a party win in American politics if it has contempt for the judgment of the American people? It can't.

The greatest political deficiency of the Republican Party today is lack of respect for the common sense of the American people. "Respect" in this context does not mean following polls or focus groups or putting one's finger slavishly to the winds. It means that what is right politically (within a constitutional framework and consistent with deeply held principles) produces electoral majorities.

Liberals also fail to understand this. But they have been fortunate to have had in Bill Clinton a leader who does, who disregards their advice, and who uses his power as the head of their party to force them to pay heed to the voice of the people. The reason Bill Clinton survived his impeachment, riding high in the polls, is that he understood what the electorate wanted and gave it to them (or at least made them think he had).

Despite the most deeply flawed presidency in the twentieth century and the worst White House scandal since Watergate, Clinton was able to sustain his popularity by remaking the Democratic Party both tactically and ideologically, much against its will. While the liberal majority in his party dug in their heels and opposed free trade, welfare reform, balanced budgets, and a tough stance on crime, Clinton pursued a "triangulation" strategy with Republicans to do just the opposite.

As a result, in the mind of the public, Clinton Democrats appear to be the party of economic vibrancy, anticrime laws, welfare reform laws, budget surpluses, and free trade. That is what the American people want, and that is what they believe Clinton has delivered. Unless Republicans change their strategy and tactics to adapt to this reality, they are destined for political irrelevance. They cannot fight past wars and expect to win present battles.

Republicans will ask how can we in good conscience respect the judgment of the American people when they failed to support the impeachment and removal of a corrupt president? The question, of course, is rhetorical. The only possible answer is: Blame the people. But if conservatives really believe in America's constitutional order, their first political article of faith surely must be this: The people are sovereign.

Where complex issues of government, society, and law are concerned, truth is elusive. Conservatives ought to know that no one has a monopoly on truth, least of all politicians in government. Should the president be impeached? Is the minimum wage a boon to workers, or does it eliminate jobs? We think we know what is true, but we also know that we may be wrong. This humility is what makes conservatives, or should make them, democrats (lower case). We do not believe in rule by the anointed; we do not believe in the divine right of the infallible.

Democracy arbitrates life's uncertainties through electoral pluralities. In America, nobody gets to decide what is true and what is false, what is right and what is wrong without the consent—or at least the tolerance—of a plurality of the American electorate. If the electorate is wrong, only the electorate can remedy its error. Hence, appropriate respect for the people's judgment is a moral imperative as well as a political necessity. If you do not have faith in the long-term good sense of the American public, then you do not really have faith in the system the Founders established. If the Founders had not had that original faith in the ultimate good sense of the American people, they would never have adopted a Constitution resting on the idea that sovereignty resides in its will.

It's the Politics, Stupid

During the impeachment debate, the American people knew that Bill Clinton was corrupt and despised him as a person even as they did not want him removed from office. Most Americans knew he was guilty of perjury, but they were reluctant to see him impeached. Clinton escaped judgment because he based his defense on conservative principles and because Republicans were silent for eight crucial months and allowed him to define the issues. When Republicans finally found their collective voice, they talked past the immediate concerns of the American electorate and based their prosecution on issues that were too complex for the public to digest.

It's the politics, stupid.

For eight months between the time that Monica Lewinsky surfaced and President Clinton admitted their relationship, Republicans said nothing about the developing sex scandal. Meanwhile, the White House launched its own national campaign to define the issues for the American public. Republican silence was based on the hope that Clinton Democrats would self-destruct and the fear that Republicans could not handle the issue without shooting themselves in the foot. The two sentiments had the same reasoning behind them: Republicans were afraid to fight the political battle. It was because Republicans did not trust themselves to frame the scandal to their advantage that they hoped for a Democratic implosion.

In political warfare, if only one side is shooting, the other side will soon be dead. While Republicans vacated the battlefield from January to August 1999, the president's allies portrayed him as a victim of government abuse. They defined the issues surrounding the investigation as government invasion of privacy (a conservative principle) and government prosecutors out of control (a conservative concern). That Americans responded to this appeal should have been cause for conservative satisfaction, not dismay. It is not the American people that Republicans should blame for their failure to remove the president. They should blame their own political ineptitude.

When Republicans finally did make their case, they built their arguments on legalistic grounds that were either unintelligible to the majority of the electorate or were based on liberal principles they had themselves previously opposed—and which the public rejected.

Although impeachment is a political process conducted by the legislative branch, Republicans notably failed to focus on the *political* case for the removal of the president (the China foreign policy scandal would have been the obvious issue). Instead, Republicans relied on interpretations of the law and on legal arguments arising from the failed Paula Jones suit to make their case for removal.

A sexual harassment statute allowing the court to investigate the personal sexual histories of defendants in sexual harassment cases led to the discovery of Monica Lewinsky. This was actually a radical law that departs from the norms of American justice, which previously enshrined the principle that a defendant is presumed innocent until proven guilty. Even accused killers have the right to be tried on the charges at hand rather than for what they may have been convicted of doing in the past. But radical sexual harassment law allows courts to dredge up not only past convictions (of which Clinton had none), but past alleged crimes as well. Once allegations are introduced into the record, and a "pattern" is established, the presumption of guilt can become overwhelming—which is why American law, before it was traduced by feminist theories, ruled out such practices.

"Sexual McCarthyism"—a charge that Democrats successfully used against the Republican prosecutors—was an invention of the radical left. Sexual harassment laws were designed by radical feminists, while conservatives opposed them. As a consequence of Republicans' folly in embracing their enemies' philosophy, the entire impeachment debate was framed by sexual harassment laws.

Furthermore, the impeachment debate revolved around questions only constitutional experts and trial lawyers could properly discuss with any claim to authority (Was the president's testimony in a sexual harassment case material or not? Was testimony in that same case about matters that should be private? What constitutes perjury? Are civil cases of perjury normally prosecuted? What is obstruction? What are impeachable offenses? Has the bar for an impeachable offense been set high enough in this case?). Because the debate was legalistic, many people thought it was just plain irrelevant, particularly since Republicans were constantly reminding them that impeachment was a political process and that political jurors would render the verdict.

In other words, Republicans chose to fight on grounds where the public could not (or would not) follow them. Because the *legalistic* arguments of the Republicans failed to gain traction with a majority of the public, the Democrats' *political* arguments prevailed. The president's privacy had been invaded; government prosecutors had abused their power; a sex act was not a reason to remove a president the people had elected. A skeptical public was readily persuaded that the president was a victim of partisan attacks. In political terms, "victims" are underdogs, little guys, that is, the people themselves. In a democratic political contest, the winner is the one who persuades the people to identify with him. In a democracy, this is the first—and perhaps only—principle of political war: The side of the underdog, which is the side of the people, wins.

In the impeachment conflict, sound Democratic political strategy was reinforced by a full-employment economy, a soaring Dow, positive social trends (declining crime rates, increasing morality indices), and no clear political framing of the case for removal. In these circumstances, the public's (conservative) response of sticking with a twice-elected sitting president was perfectly understandable, even reassuring.

Of course, the Democratic campaign in defense of the president was a remarkable display of hypocrisy and double-talk, which is to say it was a virtuoso demonstration of how a purely political strategy was able to serve a political party in grave difficulty. Thanks to a superior grasp of political strategy, the actual inventors of sexual McCarthyism (remember the hounding of Justice Clarence Thomas?) were able to pin the same charge on Republicans. Liberals who had spent four decades rewriting the Constitution suddenly emerged as the champions of original intent ("the Constitutional bar for high crimes has not been met"). The veterans of half a century of antiwar crusades against the American military became overnight enthusiasts of wag-the-dog missile strikes in the Sudan, Afghanistan, and Iraq. The creators of the special prosecutor's office, who had ruthlessly used its powers to persecute three Republican presidents, became instant critics of prosecutorial excess and the loudest proponents of reform.

As the party of bankrupt principles, discredited policies, and two-faced political arguments, the Democrats have dramatically demonstrated how effective the art of political war can be in the hands of a party that understands its principles. In contract, an illustration of Republicans' idea of political warfare is the following slogan posted on a closed-circuit television program which the Republican Policy Committee produces for House members: "Republicans target the problems; Democrats target the politics."

There could hardly be a more succinct explanation of why Republicans are so regularly routed by their Democratic adversaries in battles like the impeachment process. It's the politics, stupid. If you do not focus on winning the political battle, you do not get to target the problems.

Before Republicans can begin to change this situation, they need to stop whining that life is unfair, that Bill Clinton "stole" their programs, and that Democrats do not play by the rules. They need to stop complaining that Democrats are unprincipled or that they follow a party line. (Of course they do. It's the politics, stupid.) They need to accept that Democrats are going to practice the politics of personal destruction and attribute to Republicans the sins they themselves have committed. They do it because that is the way they win.

When Republicans complain about forces they cannot control, they behave like victims and give up the power to determine their fate. Democrats will be Democrats. They will be unprincipled and lie. Republicans can hope Democrats will behave better than this, but if Republicans go into battle expecting Democrats to be better than they are, they will only set themselves up for political ambush. Instead of complaining about others, Republicans should be asking themselves: How do they do it? How do they get away with it? What do they know that makes them able to package a bankrupt political agenda and sell it successfully to the American voter?

THE PRINCIPLES

Here are the principles of political war that the left understands, but conservatives do not:

1. Politics is war conducted by other means.
2. Politics is a war of position.
3. In political warfare, the aggressor usually prevails.
4. Position is defined by fear and hope.
5. The weapons of politics are symbols evoking fear and hope.
6. Victory lies on the side of the people.

First, a caveat. Politics is contextual: rules cannot be applied rigidly and succeed. If it is true that the aggressor usually prevails, there are times when he will not, and it is absolutely crucial to recognize them. If politics is war, it is also true that a war mentality produces sanctimony and self-serious moralizing, which can be deadly. To be effective, you need to get serious and lighten up at the same time. If politics is war, it is also a combination of blackjack, craps, and poker. Politically, it is better to be seen as a peacemaker than as a warmonger. But it is not always possible. If forced to fight, then fight to win.

1. Politics is war conducted by other means.

In political warfare you do not fight just to prevail in an argument, but to destroy the enemy's fighting ability. Republicans often seem to regard political combats as they would a debate before the Oxford Political Union, as though winning depended on rational arguments and carefully articulated principles. But the audience of politics is not made up of Oxford dons, and the rules are entirely different.

You have only thirty seconds to make your point. Even if you had time to develop an argument, the audience you need to reach (the undecided and those in the middle who are not paying much attention) would not get it. Your words would go over some of their heads and the rest would not even hear them (or quickly forget) amidst the bustle and pressure of daily life. Worse, while you have been making your argument the other side has already painted you as a mean-spirited, borderline racist controlled by religious zealots, securely in the pockets of the rich. Nobody who sees you this way is going to listen to you in any case. You are politically dead.

Politics is war. Don't forget it.

2. *Politics is a war of position.*

In war there are two sides: friends and enemies. Your task is to define yourself as the friend of as large a constituency as possible compatible with your principles, while defining your opponent as the enemy whenever you can. The act of defining combatants is analogous to the military concept of choosing the terrain of battle. Choose the terrain that makes the fight as easy for you as possible. But be careful. American politics takes place in a pluralistic framework, where constituencies are diverse and often in conflict. "Fairness" and "tolerance" are the formal rules of democratic engagement. If you appear mean-spirited or too judgmental, your opponent will more easily define you as a threat, and therefore as "the enemy" (see principle 4).

3. *In political warfare, the aggressor usually prevails.*

Republicans often pursue a conservative strategy of waiting for the other side to attack. In football, this is known as a "prevent defense." In politics it is the strategy of losers.

Aggression is advantageous because politics is a war of position, which is defined by images that stick. By striking first, you can define the issues as well as your adversary. Defining the opposition is the decisive move in all political war. Other things being equal, whoever is on the defensive generally loses.

In attacking your opponent, take care to do it effectively. "Going negative" increases the risk of being defined as an enemy. Therefore, it can be counterproductive. Ruling out the negative, however, can incur an even greater risk. In the last California senatorial election, Barbara Boxer—one of the most left-wing Democrats (in fact, the number one spender in the entire Congress)—crushed a bland, moderate Republican. Matt Fong was so moderate he was able to get the endorsement of the leading liberal papers—the *Los Angeles Times* and the *San Francisco Chronicle* (the first time they had endorsed a statewide Republican candidate since the 1960s)—and was running ahead in the polls. But Boxer went negative and Fong did not. As a result, Boxer was able to define herself as the moderate and Fong as the extremist. The American public favors the center. The decision to avoid the negative did not save Matt Fong from being defined by his opponent as mean-spirited. But it did cost him the election. Never say "never" in political battles. It is an art, not a science.

4. Position is defined by fear and hope.

The twin emotions of politics are fear and hope. Those who provide people with hope become their friends; those who inspire fear become enemies. Of the two, hope is the better choice. By offering people hope and yourself as its provider, you show your better side and maximize your potential support.

But fear is a powerful and indispensable weapon. If your opponent defines you negatively enough, he will diminish your ability to offer hope. This is why Democrats are so determined to portray Republicans as mean-spirited and hostile to minorities, the middle class, and the poor.

The smear campaign against Clarence Thomas, for example, was designed to taint all black Republicans. It was a warning to other blacks who might stray from the Democratic fold. Without their captive black constituency—the most powerful symbol of their concern for the victimized—Democrats would be dead at the polls. They would lose every major urban center and become a permanent political minority. Democrats exploit their image as the party of blacks to stigmatize Republicans as the party of racists. The success of these tactics means that as a Republican you may have a lot to offer African Americans and other minorities, but you will have to work extra hard to get anyone to listen.

Democrats have successfully associated the Religious Right with moralistic intolerance. They have been helped by intolerant pronouncements from religious leaders and by political groups with politically toxic names like the "Moral Majority" and the "Christian Coalition." As a result, it is easy for liberals to portray them as a threat to any constituency that does not share their values: "They will impose their morals on you." It does not matter whether this is true or not. Once a negative image has taken hold, the target is wounded—often mortally—in the political battle.

To combat this form of attack, it is important to work away from the negative image your opponent wants to pin on you. If you know you are going to be attacked as morally imperious, it is a good idea to lead with a position that is inclusive and tolerant. If you are going to be framed as mean-spirited and ungenerous, it is a good idea to put on a smile and lead with acts of generosity and charity. This will provide a shield from attack. When Clinton signed the welfare reform bill he made sure he was flanked by two welfare mothers.

Symbols are so powerful that if you manipulate them cleverly, as Democrats do, you can even launch mean-spirited attacks on your opponents and pretend to be compassionate while doing it. Democrats understand, for example, that positioning themselves as victims gives them a license to attack. A gay politician like Barney Frank can assault an opponent and call it self-defense. The president's wife can issue McCarthy-like proclamations about a "vast right wing conspiracy" and get away with it because she is a woman and the first lady, and because she has allies like James Carville and Sidney Blumenthal who will make her aggression look like self-defense. In the same way, Democrats rely on black extremists like Maxine Waters to slander Republicans as racists.

But remember this: using fear as a weapon can be dangerous. Enemies inspire fear; friends do not. That is why Clinton lets his surrogates do the dirty work. When and how to use fear is a political art. If you are a white male in a culture whose symbols have been defined by liberals, be careful when you go on the offensive, and be sure to surround yourself with allies who are neither male nor white.

5. The weapons of politics are symbols evoking fear and hope.

The most important symbol is the candidate. Does the candidate, in his own person, inspire fear or hope? Voters want to know: Is the candidate someone who cares about people like me? Do I feel good about him, or does he put me on guard? Would I want to sit next to him at dinner? Style, especially for high public office, is as important as any issue or strategy. Jack Kennedy—a relatively inexperienced, do-nothing congressman and senator—was able to win a national election merely by reciting problems and then repeating the litany "we can do bettah." Why? In part it was because he was handsome, witty, young, and charming—and was not a zealot.

Republicans lose a lot of political battles because they come across as hard-edged, scolding, scowling, and sanctimonious. A good rule of thumb is to be just the opposite. You must convince people you care about them before they will care about what you have to say. When you speak, do not forget that a sound bite is all you have. Whatever you have to say, make sure to say it loud and clear. Keep it simple and keep it short—a slogan is always better. Repeat it often. Put it on television. Radio is good, but with few exceptions, only television reaches a public that is electorally significant. In politics, television is reality.

Of course, you have a base of supporters who will listen for hours to what you have to say if that is what you want. In the battles facing you, they will play an important role. Therefore, what you say to them is also important. But it is not going to decide elections. The audiences that will determine your fate are audiences that you will first have to persuade. You will have to find a way to reach them, get them to listen, and then to support you. With these audiences, you will never have time for real arguments or proper analyses. Images—symbols and sound bites—will always prevail. Therefore, it is absolutely essential to focus your message and repeat it over and over again. For a candidate this means the strictest discipline. Lack of focus will derail your message. If you make too many points, your message will be diffused and nothing will get through. The result will be the same as if you had made no point at all.

The same is true for the party as a whole. Democrats have a party line. When they are fighting an issue they focus their agenda. Every time a Democrat steps in front of the cameras there is at least one line in his speech that is shared with his colleagues. "Tax breaks for the wealthy at the expense of the poor" is one example. Repetition insures that the message will get through. When Republicans speak, they all march to a different drummer. There are many messages instead of one. One message is a sound bite. Many messages are a confusing noise.

Symbols and sound bites determine the vote. These are what hit people in the gut before they have time to think. And these are what people remember. Symbols are the impressions that last, and therefore that ultimately define you. Carefully chosen words and phrases are more important than paragraphs, speeches, party platforms and manifestos. What you project through images is what you are.

The faces that represent Republicans are also images. In a pluralistic community, diversity is important. Currently, too many Republican faces (what you see on your television screen) are Southern white men.

America is based on the idea that individual merit is what counts. As conservators of the American principle, we reject artificial diversity and racial quotas. But this is political warfare. Images are what count. The image is the medium, and the medium is the message. Therefore, diversity is more than important. It is crucial to becoming a national majority. But it is also crucial because it is just. As conservatives, as defenders of America's democratic principle, we want every constituency to feel included.

6. Victory lies on the side of the people.

This is the bottom line for each of the principles and for all of the principles. You must define yourself in ways that people understand. You must give people hope in your victory, and make them fear the victory of your opponent. You can accomplish both by identifying yourself and your issues with the underdog and the victim, with minorities and the disadvantaged, with the ordinary Janes and Joes.

This is what Democrats do best, and Republicans often neglect to do at all. Every political statement by a Democratic is an effort to say: "Democrats care about women, children, minorities, working Americans, and the poor; Republicans are mean-spirited, serve the rich, and don't care about you." This is the Democrats' strategy of political war. If Republicans are to win the political war and become a national majority they have to turn these images around.

They also have to make their campaigns a cause. During the Cold War, Republicans had a cause. They were saving the country from Communism, and—in its later decades—from leftist appeasers. The cause resonated at every level with the American people. The poorest citizens understood that their freedom was at stake in electing Republicans to conduct the nation's defense.

In a democracy, the cause that fires up passions is the cause of the people. That is why politicians like to run "against Washington" and against anything that represents the "powers that be." As the left has shown, the idea of justice is a powerful motivator. It will energize the troops and fuel the campaigns that are necessary to win the political war. Republicans believe in economic opportunity and individual freedom. The core of their ideas is justice for all. If they could make this intelligible to the American electorate, they would make themselves the party of the American people.

The Practice

Those are the principles. Here are some examples of the ways they work (and do not work).

Truth in Labeling

"Tax breaks for the wealthy on the backs of the poor" is the Democratic sound bite that defines Republicans as mean-spirited fatcats and enemies of the poor. It is a lie that has been imprinted on the electorate through a million repetitions. It is the chant of every Democrat in Congress and every Democratic pundit in the media.

What is the Republican chant? There is none.

The first new weapon Republicans need in their arsenal is a sound bite that defines the Democrats and neutralizes this attack. The Democratic slogan is effective because it applies all the principles: It is not an argument that can be refuted; it is an image that imprints itself on the mind as a self-evident whole. It defines Republicans as selfish, mean-spirited, and corrupt. It defines Republicans as enemies of the people. It does not have to be defended because it does not bother to justify itself.

An image or a sound bite is the crucial form of political firepower. It is a voter-seeking missile. If amplified by television or radio, it is like a cruise missile that can go hundreds, even thousands, of miles to hit an individual target. Think of yourself as separated from the electorate by oceans of static. Local and international news, family matters, work demands, business affairs, entertainment, and other distractions all clutter the airwaves between you and the voters. The sound bite, like a cruise missile, gets through. That is what makes it decisive.

Neither counterargument nor reason can combat the Democrats' class-warfare missile. The people the Democrats' sound bite reaches will never hear the counterargument or the evidence that refutes the Democratic smear. The static is too great; the clutter is too dense. Never underestimate the difficulty of reaching the people with a political message. The only effective response to a sound bite is another sound bite, a political cruise missle.

Here is a suggestion for the Republican sound bite: "Taxes for bureaucrats out of the pockets of the people."

This is an answer to the Democrats. Nothing longer will do the job. "Taxes for bureaucrats out of the pockets of the people" sums up what Democratic policies are all about. If the trillions spent by the welfare state went to poor people instead of to bureaucrats, there would be no poor people; if the education billions went to the classroom and paid teachers to teach (instead of merely to show up for the job), there would be no education crisis.

The sound bite principle can be applied to other political issues as well. Republicans should label their bills with language that gives them an advantage. Unfortunately, Republicans do not pay enough attention to details like this. Take the Republicans' "Education Savings Bill," which failed to pass in the 1998 legislative session. Its very name projects an image of frugality that fits the Democrats' negative image of Republicans as mean-spirited accountants. "Education Savings Bill" sounds like the idea of stingy people: "Let's spend less on education." In labeling their bill, Republicans did the Democrats' work for them. They reinforced a negative image and made themselves targets even before the Democrats got around to attacking the Education Savings Bill—as a "tax break for the wealthy on the backs of the poor."

Wealthy people, of course, do not need a tax break to send their children to private school. Working Americans do. So why not say so? Why not call this legislation the "Working Americans Education Bill?" And why not remind voters every chance you get that it is well-heeled Democratic legislators who send their own children to private schools while denying working Americans and the poor the same privilege. Republicans complain that Democrats use the politics of "class warfare" against them, but Democrats will use class warfare as long as it works. The only way to stop them is to turn it around. *Taxes for bureaucrats out of the pockets of the people*: "The Democrats' policies mean private schools for the liberal elites and educational squalor for working Americans." *That* is a voter-seeking missile.

There's a profound difference between "policy" and "politics"—a distinction that is often lost on Republicans. A good policy is not automatically good politics, especially if it is easily misrepresented by the opposition and hard to explain to the ordinary voter. A good policy can become bad politics if is identified with the wrong spokesman.

Consider Steve Forbes's flat-tax proposal, which would tax everyone at a uniform rate of 17 percent with no loopholes. It is probably a good idea. It eliminates large bureaucracies, provides an across-the-board tax cut, and allows taxpayers to know exactly how much the government is taking from them.

But look who's presenting it. Steve Forbes is personally worth more than four hundred million dollars. That easily puts him in the bracket of those who currently pay 39.6 percent. His tax plan would cut his contribution to the "general welfare" by nearly 23 percent. But someone in the 18 percent bracket would only get a 1 percent cut under his plan. Forbes's personal cut would be millions of dollars. How is Steve Forbes going to sell a tax cut for himself that exceeds the entire income most Americans? He cannot.

The only reason Steve Forbes lasted so long as a candidate is that he never had to run against a Democrat. Republicans were not going to indulge in class-warfare rhetoric against him. Democrats will. "Mr. Forbes, would you tell Americans how you can justify a multimillion dollar tax rebate for yourself. On your website you say a family of four earning thirty-six thousand dollars will get "a tax cut of more than sixteen *hundred* dollars"—while you get *millions*. Now how can that be just? Or fair? Or American?

There is no answer that Steve Forbes can give in thirty seconds to convince the great mass of voters who are earning average incomes that Steve Forbes cares about them. Forbes has another problem. He has an owlish look and a cerebral personality. He lacks personal warmth. He is not "one of the guys"—someone you expect to meet in the local bar or bowling alley. This is as great a problem as his wealth in connecting with average voters and leaving the impression that he can understand and care about their problems.

Steve Forbes can never go anywhere as a candidate, although none of his well-paid professional political staffers will tell him so. If Forbes really wanted to change the tax system he should have taken the fifty million dollars or more he has spent on the impossible task of electing himself and used it to elect others to do the job he wants done. The tax issue is a real problem for Republicans. Every across-the-board tax cut is going to benefit the upper income brackets because they pay at a higher rate and bear a greater weight of the tax burden.

Issues and bills are not the only items that can be labeled to positive effect. Individuals and parties can as well. Of course, it is difficult to label a whole party, so Democrats seize on a radical wing of the Republican Party and say that the party itself is a captive of its extreme element. The "Christian Right" has been demonized by liberal activists and has become a symbol of intolerance, zealotry, and hostility to minorities. Liberals then use the Christian Right to demonize the Republican Party as a whole.

So adept are Democrats in applying stigmas to their Republican opponents that they do not even need to use the words "Christian Right" to achieve their goal. Consider a typical mailer signed by California senator Barbara Boxer to solicit funds for the opponent of Republican congressman James Rogan. Rogan was targeted by Democrats because he was one of the House managers of the impeachment process. Before becoming a Republican, Rogan had been a John F. Kennedy Democrat and a member of the central committee of the California Democratic Party. He has explained that he switched parties because of the leftward swing of the Democrats rather than because of any dramatic changes in his own views. In 1999, he defied the Republican chairman of the judiciary committee, who was his mentor, and opposed a bill the chairman had authored that would have restricted the sexual content of Hollywood films. Yet Boxer wrote: "You may not have heard of Congressman James Rogan before the impeachment. But take it from me, the impeachment trial was not an aberration in Rogan's career. James Rogan is one of the most radical right-wing members of Congress."

Typically, the Republican response to such attacks is tentative and defensive—"I am not an extremist"—and hence doomed to failure. Democrats label Republicans "right-wing," meaning "intolerant, extreme." Of course, it is difficult, if not impossible, to disprove a negative. While you are busy defending yourself, the opposition is on the attack. That is why the best defense is always an offense. But you cannot have an offense unless you are armed, and Republicans have no corresponding label to pin on Democrats.

Is this because the Democratic Party has no radical wing? Hardly. There is a militant left in the Democratic Party that has enormous influence and includes the likes of Maxine Waters, Barney Frank, James Carville, and Sidney Blumenthal. During the Clinton years, forty members of the congressional Black Caucus signed a "covenant" with America's leading racist and Jew-hater, Louis Farrakhan, but Republicans made nothing of this at the time, and it is now forgotten. Yet a single speaking engagement by Representative Bob Barr or Senator Trent Lott to the obscure "Conservative Citizens Councils," associated in name and some personnel with the long defunct White Citizens Councils, can be effectively used by Democrats to tar Republicans and accuse them of consorting with racists.

There is also a large socialist wing of the Democratic coalition (although only a few members would publicly identify themselves as such). Government unions that represent teachers and public employees are not only living conflicts of interest (special interests that elect their own employers and lobby to raise their own salaries). They are also the socialist vanguards of the Democratic Party, whose only consistent agenda is to expand big government. In addition, fifty-eight congressional Democrats have identified themselves as a "Progressive Caucus," which is formally allied with the "Democratic Socialists" and other organizations of the radical left.

It is not hard to come up with a label for Democrats: Leftists. The Democratic Party is a party of the Left.

But nobody calls Democrats leftists, even though Republicans are casually identified as right-wingers by Democracts and the press. Even Republicans collude in the cover-up and join the charade when they call Democrats "liberals" rather than leftists. "Liberal" is a word whose root is "liberty," not "government control," which is the Democrats' agenda. (In what ways are modern liberals "liberal" in any case, except in their attitudes towards drugs and sex?) We need a truth-in-labeling law for political parties. But Republicans should not wait for others to make the correction. They should employ "left," and "radical left," and "far left" as reflexive labels for describing those who belong to what is now called the "liberal" wing of the Democratic Party.

Leftists have a history that accurately links them to experiments in big government and socialist solutions. The word "liberal," on the other hand, misleadingly connects them to Adam Smith, James Madison, and John Locke. These were the philosophical champions of free markets and political democracy, not government control and economic leveling. Republican legislators should practice referring to Democrats like Maxine Waters as "my opponent from the far left," and to "my left-wing colleagues Bernie Sanders and Barney Frank." They should stop blaming the media for describing leftists as "liberals," while letting them off the hook themselves.

The Destruction of Newt Gingrich

The Democrats' destruction of Newt Gingrich was a classic example of successful political warfare. It had nothing to do with intellectual argument or political principle, nor could it. You cannot cripple an opponent by outwitting him in a political debate; you can do it only by following Lenin's injunction: "In political conflicts, the goal is not to refute your opponent's argument, but to wipe him from the face of the earth." We do not go as far as Lenin, but destroying an opponent's effectiveness is a fairly common practice. Personal smears accomplish this, and Democrats are very good at them.

Newt Gingrich was something rare in Republican politics—a genuine movement leader. The electoral victory Gingrich spearheaded in 1994 was the result of more than a decade of organizing a grassroots political movement, selecting and training candidates, and shaping a political message. It was actually more than a political message: it was a call to transform government; it was an inspiring political vision.

For that very reason Gingrich had to be neutralized. Even before he became speaker, Gingrich had been targeted as the most effective Republican leader, and therefore as someone who had to be destroyed. "Newt is the nerve center and the energy source," explained a Democratic strategist who understood political warfare. "Going after him is like taking out command and control."

While Gingrich extended an olive branch to Democrats in his inaugural speech as speaker, it was the Democrats' goal to cripple Gingrich, and then to kill him politically—to drive him from the field of battle. The centerpiece of the Democrats' attack was a campaign of slander capped by an Ethics Committee ruling that would tar him permanently as unworthy. It succeeded, on a spurious pretext, in a congress that Republicans controlled. The Ethics Committee finding—that Gingrich had violated the House rules—provided a "fact" that appeared to validate the Democrats' slander. It allowed them to make Gingrich into the enemy of good government—and hence an enemy of the people. It was tantamount to political death.

The keys to this result were the ethics charges that the Democrats filed almost from the day he took office. Eventually, Democrats lodged seventy-four separate charges against Gingrich, sixty-five of which were summarily "laughed out of committee." The number of charges was itself significant, revealing how thoroughly it was a case of "show me the man and I'll find you the crime."

In similar circumstances, Republicans would never think to file charges they knew had no chance of sticking, let alone charges that were phony. But Democrats understood that the charges were filed in public but discarded in private—or at least where the public would not pay attention to them. Even though they were thrown out, the charges themselves were useful. Some of the mud inevitably stuck to the target. The blows steadily weakened Gingrich, making it harder for him to defend himself. The sheer number of charges kept Gingrich—normally an aggressive leader—off balance and on the defensive.

Eventually, the feckless Republicans on the Ethics Committee caved to the Democrats, and Gingrich was forced to concede to one frivolous charge. But that was enough. The Speaker was assessed a three-hundred-thousand-dollar fine. Three years later, the IRS cleared Gingrich of the concocted charge, but the battle was long over. Gingrich was no longer speaker. He had been tainted as a man with poor ethical standards and permanently crippled, and the Republicans and the country had lost a leader.

What could the Republicans have done? They could have remembered that they were in a war. They could have responded in kind to this blatant attempt to destroy their leader. Instead of standing around and watching him pecked to death, they could have created a war room and a plan to fight back. The day the first charge was filed against Newt Gingrich by David Bonior, the Democratic whip (and a charter member of the party's militant left), the Republicans should have filed their first charge against Bonior. And then they should have filed charge for charge until the Democrats gave up their attack.

The Democrats employed the same aggressive and unprincipled assault to neutralize the investigation of President Clinton by special prosecutor Kenneth Starr. They attacked the special prosecutor and put him on the defensive. They attacked him relentlessly until every word and every charge he made became automatically suspect in the eyes of the electorate; the polls reflected the success of the Democrats' efforts. Their attack strategy was the political equivalent of an antimissile defense. If Republicans had fought with half the tenacity to defend an innocent leader that Democrats did to defend a guilty president, the political landscape today would be dramatically different.

Winning with a Losing Issue

With a proper strategy you can even win an election with a "third-rail" issue in a losing state. The November 1998 elections in California were an unmitigated disaster for the Republican Party, a defeat unparalleled in the state since the 1930s. The Republican gubernatorial candidate lost to his opponent by twenty points, taking down virtually the entire slate. After sixteen years of Republican domination, only two Republicans won (minor) statewide offices.

The results in the Hispanic community were even worse than in the general population. Hispanic mistrust of Republicans deepened over two elections as a result of anti-illegal immigrant ballot initiatives. This alienation was registered in the fact that in 1998 the Republican gubernatorial candidate got only 17 percent to 23 percent of the Hispanic vote (depending on the exit poll). This disastrous showing occurred in spite of the fact that the statewide Republican campaign was better financed than the Democratic opposition, spending forty-three million dollars to thirty-three million dollars; in spite of the fact that Republicans ran more Hispanic candidates than Democrats; and in spite of the fact that the Republican gubernatorial candidate made an extra effort in the Hispanic community, including a television ad campaign on Spanish-language television.

But five months earlier, a ballot initiative sponsored by Republican Ron Unz on an Hispanic issue, in the same state, had an exactly opposite result. Unz's initiative to end bilingual education was denounced by every major newspaper and establishment figure in California, by the chairmen of both the Republican and Democratic parties, by every Democract, and by the Republican candidate for governor. The antibilingual campaign was only able to raise 1.5 million dollars and could not finance a single television ad, while the opposition spent 4.8 million dollars and financed a strong television advertising campaign. Yet, despite these enormous obstacles, the antibilingual campaign succeeded in a landslide victory, with 61 percent voting for and only 39 percent against. The initiative received 35 percent of the Hispanic vote—twice what the Republican gubernatorial candidate would receive five months later.

How could this happen? The answer is that the sponsors of the antibilingual initiative followed the principles of political war, especially the most basic: positioning yourself on the side of the people. They defined themselves as friends of Hispanic children who were trying to learn English and better their lives. As a result, they won the sympathy and support not only of Hispanics who wanted their children to have a chance in life, but of all those who saw immigrant children as society's underdogs deserving a fair shake.

At the first press conference, Unz and his cosponsors said they were responding to a recent demonstration by Hispanic parents at city hall. Hispanic parents had organized a protest to demand their children be taught in English, a privilege that the current "bilingual" programs required by the school district denied them. As studies had revealed, the bilingual education programs mandated by the school system were primarily jobs programs for Spanish-speaking adults. They were monolingual not bilingual, and most of the children enrolled in them never learned English. The Hispanic demonstrators wanted their children withdrawn from these Spanish-language programs so they could be taught in English and one day get decent jobs and a shot at the American dream. Sponsors of the antibilingual initiative present at the press conference along with Unz were an Hispanic teacher-activist and an Episcopal nun who had run her own program to teach Hispanic children English.

There were many arguments that could have been made for teaching Hispanic immigrants English. Bilingualism could legitimately be seen as a threat to national unity. Canada is a ready-to-hand example of what can happen to a country with more than one official language. But such a positioning of the initiative would have invited the response that it was anti-immigrant and would persecute a vulnerable segment of the community (poor immigrant children). This would have played into the hands of the left-wing opposition and would have made it easy for them to portray the sponsors and the initiative as enemies of children, minorities, and the poor. Positioned that way, the initiative would have failed.

But once its image as a helping hand to a disadvantaged group was established in the mind of the California electorate, victory was assured. Early polls taken before the opposition was able to mount its smear campaign showed the initiative winning 80 percent overall and 83 percent of Hispanic voters. Not even a 4.8 million-dollar campaign smearing its proponents as "xenophobes" and "racists" could whittle that figure to below 60 percent. This is what a strategically sound position on the battlefield can accomplish.

Compassionate Conservatism

When Democrats speak politically, every other word is an appeal to "women," "children," "minorities," "working Americans," or "the poor." This immediately prepares the battleground in a way that favors their victory. All Americans regard themselves as underdogs: just ask Bill Gates; to care about minorities and the vulnerable is to care about *them*. Most Americans are tolerant and compassionate: to care about minorities and the vulnerable is to resonate with Americans' sense of their better selves. Taking the side of the angels is good when you are going into the political battle.

Another advantage of the Democrats' rhetoric is that it speaks directly to the American people about things they understand—the concrete lives of their fellow human beings. Speaking about women, children, minorities, working Americans, and the poor makes the connection. It establishes a link between speaker and listener, appearing to come from the heart. If it comes across sincerely, it immediately identifies the speaker as a friend. Republicans, by contrast, tend to speak in abstract language about legalistic doctrines and economic budgets. They sound like businessmen, lawyers, and accountants. They argue the virtues of flat taxes versus value-added taxes. They talk about capital gains tax cuts. They speak from the head instead of the heart.

Most Americans do not know what "capital" is, let alone a capital gain. If you had an hour (instead of thirty seconds) and were able to explain to them why a capital gains tax might be a double tax, it would probably make no difference at all. When you were finished most of them would shrug their shoulders and say "Let them pay it anyway. They're rich enough." They have no idea of how the economy works, what an incentive system is, or why the stock market is more than a gambling casino. Talk about capital gains tax cuts is only important to those who understand them, and they are already mostly Republicans.

Democrats know how to use a budget to reach people's hearts. Defeat at the hands of the Democrats in the 1998 budget negotiations was a political backbreaker for Republicans and cost them many votes in the congressional elections that followed. In the fall of 1998, Bill Clinton was a wounded president and a figure of national disgust. But his political strategy going into the budget negotiations was classic: he positioned himself as a defender of the vulnerable and the weak; he positioned his opponents as uncaring advocates of the greedy and the strong.

"We have a budget surplus for the first time in a generation," President Clinton might have said. "Let's show that we care. Let's give a billion dollars to the children. Better yet, so that everybody will notice our caring deed, let's break the budget caps. Let's break our promise not to spend more than we have. So let's not cut any other programs to pay for this one. Let's just add it to the education package already in the bill." His real message was this: "However bad I may be, however embarrassing and tawdry I may appear to you, remember this—I am still a caring Democrat. I am all that stands between the helpless children and these mean-spirited Republicans who would not dream of breaking the budget caps to help little children. I'm still the only hope these children have to get what they need." A winning strategy. But the only way Clinton could make the strategy work politically was if Republicans could be counted on to play their familiar role as the bad hats, the scrooges who would say: "We don't have the money."

Of course, Republicans knew that not much of Clinton's education money would reach children. It would go into the coffers of the education bureaucracy; it would line the pockets of the teachers' unions, whose members get paid (in the present union-controlled system) not for how well they teach, but just for showing up. In short, Clinton's plan was *tax money for bureaucrats out of the pockets of the people.* But even this sound bite, had the Republicans used it, would have been trumped by the sound bite Clinton was counting on: "Democrats want more money for education; Republicans want less." And that is the way it would be played. There would be no public debate. There would only be this sound bite in the morning papers and on the evening news: "President Proposes More Money For Education. Republicans Call For Less." If Republicans refused to agree to more money, they were going to lose.

So what did the Republicans do? At least they had learned enough not to say "There's no money." It is a bad answer that would have cost them dearly. What they said was "Where's the money?"—as though Clinton would have to answer. It was an improvement on past Republican performances, but the result was exactly the same.

A Clintonesque response to the Republicans' question can be easily imagined: "It's a five-hundred-billion-dollar bill we're talking about. You mean there's not an *eentsy beentsy* billion for the children?" There is no winning answer to that question. There is no answer at all. Republicans realized this within a few hours, conceded the inevitable, and signed the bill. Politically, it was a typical Republican performance: they managed to look mean-spirited, stupid, and weak, all at the same time.

What might they have done to prevent this defeat? They could have positioned themselves on the side of the children and defined their Democratic opponents as enemies of the children. They could have said: "We want ten billion dollars for the children, not the measly one billion you're suggesting. But we want it in the form of scholarships for the inner city kids you Democrats have trapped in dangerous and failing public schools." This would have rammed Clinton up against the teachers' unions, the largest special interest in the Democratic Party, and the chief opponent of reforms to improve the schools. It would have positioned Republicans as the advocates of the most disadvantaged, oppressed, and deprived of America's children. This would have exposed the Democrats (whose own children are well-taught in private schools) as hypocritical oppressors of minorities and the poor.

Why is it that no Republican ever reminds people that Democrats and liberals have controlled every major school system in the nation for more than sixty years? If there is a national education crisis, Democrats and liberals are responsible. Why should Bill Clinton, Ted Kennedy, and Jesse Jackson be able to send their children to private schools while preventing inner-city parents from having the same privilege and choice? If the disastrous condition of our schools has blighted the lives of millions upon millions of poor and minority children, liberals and Democrats are responsible. If education is the crucial ladder of immigrant success, Democrats have denied millions of immigrant children the use of that ladder.

By creating a paternalistic system that does not serve the poorest and neediest segments of society, by inflicting tax burdens and regulations that limit economic opportunity, Democrats and liberals have blighted the lives of minorities and the poor. Republicans have a solution. They intend to revive these opportunities, to liberate minorities through educational choice, through policies that restore the bottom rungs to the ladder of success. This is the message Republicans need to take to the American people, and to inner city communities. Boldly argued and vigorously advanced, these ideas can guide Republicans to a national majority.

What to Do

What general steps can be taken to reshape the Republican Party as a potential American majority?

The first would be to stop complaining that life is unfair. The press *is* outrageously biased against conservatives. Ninety percent of the Washington press corps voted for Clinton and it shows in the relentlessly liberal twist of the news as they report it. Republicans must come to terms with this reality. They have to stop whining about it and then put their minds to constructing political strategies that are based on the reality.

If the press is against you, you have to go over their heads and address the American people directly. What this means is that every major new Republican policy initiative must be accompanied by a mass media campaign of thirty-second television spots. These can be paid for by for-profit or nonprofit groups, but are absolutely necessary to create a public opinion base for conservative policy initiatives. That is the only way the spin will be to Republicans' advantage.

The Clintons' proposal for a national healthcare plan was not defeated by Republican spokesmen, but by a thirty-five-million-dollar national television advertising campaign in which "Harry and Louise" explained to Americans that the Clintons were going to take away their family doctor. That was an exemplary demonstration of how Republican views can reach the American people over the leftward spin of the mass media. Newt Gingrich's failed orphanage idea might have been helped (though probably not much) by changing the word "orphanage" to "youth care center," as some have suggested. Only a fifty-million-dollar national television campaign explaining how enlightened and progressive a "Boys Town" approach can be would do the necessary job.

Politics is a moving target. You cannot fight last year's wars and expect to win—unless your opponent is asleep at the helm. Democrats never sleep. By refashioning their agenda as one of economic buoyancy, free trade, balanced budgets, welfare reform, tough attitudes towards crime, while adding the signature Democratic concerns for women, children, minorities, working Americans, and the poor, the Clinton Democrats have made their party a much tougher opponent. What should the Republican response be?

Right now, Republicans are identified with the flat tax, opposition to minimum wage increases, opposition to more money for education, opposition to more money for healthcare and health research. If this is combined with an opposition to abortion rights, perceived intolerance to the homosexual minority, and zealous promotion of organized religion, the resulting profile is hardly the platform of a modern majority party. Such a party can no longer win a governorship in a Bible-belt state like South Carolina! And such a party loses a governorship by twenty points in the must-win state of California. In order to win now, Republican candidates have to run away from their party image, much like Democrats until Clinton's "triangulation" turned them around. The Republican Party can remake itself into a majority party by focusing on the following five agendas:

1. Military preparedness

If the Clinton Administration has demonstrated one thing, it is that Democrats cannot be trusted with the nation's security. The Clinton administration's gutting of the defense budget, its failure to build an antiballistic missile defense, its erosion of America's military credibility, and its addiction to UN and NATO diplomacy, multilateralism, arms control agreements, and other failed panaceas of the left is the result of an apparently incurable policy reflex. It is coupled with the solicitation of illegal funds from communist China to Democratic campaigns, with enormous security breaches allowed by the Clinton administration, and with irresponsible technology transfers to potential military enemies, particularly China.

These factors make security and defense the obvious central issues of a national Republican campaign. The world is a more dangerous place, despite and even because of Clinton's wanton deployments of U.S. military forces. (The Clinton deployments are four times greater than the combined deployments of the preceding fifty years, which included the Cold War.) As the Clinton presidency has amply demonstrated, Democrats lack the tough-minded realism necessary to deal with national security threats. This makes a Republican White House a national imperative.

But remember: You need a fifty-million-dollar television campaign to make real to voters that which is real in life: that American children will die and that civilization is at stake if we do not improve the military, develop an antimissile defense, and aggressively pursue our security interests.

2. Give minorities and the poor a shot at the American Dream

Welfare paternalism, regulations, taxes and quotas, excessive urban crime, lower performance expectations, and metastasizing school bureaucracies are oppressing poor people, minorities, and children, and cutting off their opportunities. Republican policies and principles— lower taxes, single standards, school choice, secure streets, and individual responsibility provide the necessary rungs in the ladder of success. Empowering minorities, poor people, and working Americans by putting the education dollar directly in their hands, either through "opportunity scholarships" or school vouchers, is the most important single legislative step that Republicans can take in liberating them from the chains with which liberals have shackled them.

3. Accountability and standards for government expenditures

Republicans are not against more money for schools. They are *for* more money for schools and against *wasting* money on schools. They want the money to go to educating the kids and not to buttressing failed school systems and lining the pockets of education bureaucrats. If Democrats propose one hundred billion dollars for school expenditures, Republicans should propose 150 billion dollars—but only for schools that implement a teacher standards test (the penalty for failure being dismissal), require an annual increase in student performance tests, abolish bilingual programs that fail to teach students English, teach phonics-based reading, do not teach "new math," and require expulsion for disruptive students.

This is the way to define a Republican education agenda. (Clinton could not sign such a bill.) Republicans will have grasped both the common sense and compassion sides of the issue.

4. Crime

This is the one issue where liberals cannot control the media spin, because local stations must report crime to keep their ratings.

In California, the left has launched a campaign against the "three-strikes law" because the third felony that sends an offender away for life can be nonviolent. Where is the Republican Party? Why is it not screaming that the American people have a right to tell a violent felon that he is on notice: if he has already committed one violent crime, another violent crime will keep him off our streets for life. Republicans should put up ballot initiatives all over the country for a two-strikes law if both felonies are violent.

Felons who use a gun to commit a crime should automatically have ten years added to their sentence. "Hard time for armed crime." Republicans should support the NRA-sponsored "exile" program to remove armed felons from law-abiding communities. The protection of lawful citizens from security threats at home and abroad is the single most important responsibility of government.

5. Individual responsibility

Individual responsibility means that individuals should win jobs and educational places on merit, not on race or gender. It is the basic American principle of nondiscrimination and fairness to all.

The Democratic Party supports racial preferences, the policy of segregationists in the era before the Civil Rights Acts. It is time to end government racial discrimination for good; it is time to restore a single standard for all Americans. This is the most basic principle of our multiethnic civic culture.

THE REPUBLICAN PARTY can be a majority party, but only if it respects the common sense of the American people, recovers the Reagan optimism ("it's morning in America"), diversifies the face it presents to the voting public, remembers that it is not simply how much you spend but how much you spend on vote-decisive activities that counts, and never forgets that the American electorate is very large and (when it comes to politics) very hard of hearing. Above all, Republicans need to remember their heritage as the party of Lincoln, of principle, of the underdog, the party of the American Dream.

OBSERVATIONS

I began this essay to solve a puzzle: How is it that Democrats are able to campaign on Republican programs and ideas—balanced budgets, welfare reform, tough attitudes towards crime and family values—and win, while Republicans who have been promoting these same principles for decades—not just during election cycles—lose? How is it that a "social issue" like education is a Democratic issue? If liberals and Democrats are responsible for the education crisis, how is it that they can claim education as their issue while Republicans cannot? My answer has been that Republicans do not understand (as Democrats do) that politics is war conducted by other means; that it is a war of position; and that you can only win by linking your agendas directly to the interests of women, children, minorities, working Americans, and the poor. In a democracy the position you want to be on is the side of the underdog, which is how most Americans identify themselves (whether they are really underdogs or not).

I have defined six principles as guides to the political battle. The fundamental principle is this: People will not care about what you have to say unless they believe you care about them. The art of politics is persuading people who do not know you, and who will never know you except through symbols and sound bites, that you care about them. Republicans do not pay enough attention to this simple truth.

Some years ago Ronald Reagan was at a meeting of Democrats and Republicans. During the proceedings, there was a pause in which both sides doodled on the pads in front of them while they waited for the talks to resume. Afterwards, a reporter collected the doodles and discovered that the Republicans had drawn geometric shapes while the Democrats had drawn animals and people's faces. Only one Republican had drawn a face—Ronald Reagan.

In political warfare, the weapons are words and symbols because there is no time to reach the electorate with lengthy arguments—or even short ones. In these circumstances a slogan, a symbol, or a gesture is all you have. A good example of how effective a symbol can be is John F. Kennedy's winning of the black vote in 1960. He did it with a single phone call to Martin Luther King in jail.

Until that moment, blacks had been suspicious of the Democratic Party because it was the party of the segregationists. Kennedy changed that with a phone call. He did not have to issue a policy statement or a position paper about racial issues. Few people would have read one if he had. Few people would have listened to any speech he might have given. The image was everything. He did not have to decide complex issues about segregation, or about states' rights, or about individual responsibilities. He had only to make a phone call.

Recently, a number of black intellectuals and political figures commented on why 90 percent of blacks give Bill Clinton their support and why many even consider him "the first black president." Although the commentators were politically savvy people, their reasons had nothing to do with the policies he has pursued, because many of these same people have viewed the same policies (like welfare reform) as "antiblack." The reasons they gave for considering Clinton a friend, and even "one of them," were that he plays the saxophone, has made a lot of black appointments, shows up in black churches, has black friends like Vernon Jordan, and generally seems comfortable around black people. These are all symbols of where Bill Clinton stands. They convey a single message: He shares things with us; he sympathizes with us; he cares about us. This message trumps any policy he has pursued or any program he has enacted.

There is another reason why Clinton has such an advantage with black voters, and he has the advantage almost for nothing: blacks perceive Republicans not only as alien to them, but actively hostile. If Republicans are not actual racists, they will associate with racists, as Bob Barr and Trent Lott are alleged to have done. Moreover, Republicans do not seem to care. A very prominent black Republican privately complained to Republican National Committee Chairman Jim Nicholson that not a single Republican member of Congress had attended commerce secretary Ron Brown's funeral. How could Republicans not have paid tribute to the first black secretary of commerce?

It is not Ron Brown's politics that caused Republicans to neglect his memorial service. After all, there were Republican legislators present at Congressman George Brown's funeral and George Brown was practically a communist. Despite their stated intentions to include blacks, Republicans do not make the gestures necessary to recruit them, to show that they care. As a result, even though Republican policies like lower taxes and school choice are beneficial to blacks, the black community is not listening. Some of Republicans' failure to reach out to African Americans is a defensive attitude caused by the attacks from the left, but this should not be used as an excuse for what is a serious Republican fault. Republicans are no more racists than Democrats are. But Republicans make almost no effort to show that they are not. With few exceptions—Jack Kemp, J. C. Watts, and George W. and Jeb Bush, for example—they make almost no effort to show that they care about what happens to people who live in our inner cities and are suffering from their malignant effects.

Republicans have appointed blacks to significant positions. But unlike Democratic appointments, theirs are often kept secret. Pete Wilson appointed a black former welfare mother to head his welfare department and preside over its reforms. Eloise Anderson is one of the most informed and successful public policy experts on welfare issues, a tough-minded conservative and a Republican who served on the welfare task forces of Governor Tommy Thompson and Newt Gingrich. Think of how powerful Eloise Anderson's voice would be on the social policy issues that are the key to Republicans winning the confidence of minorities and poor people in California. But few Californians have ever heard of Eloise Anderson, including Republicans. Pete Wilson, whose political instincts are normally sharp, kept her a virtual secret. He did not give her a public platform to make important policy announcements, or showcase her on television at state events. If a political figure is not on television making important policy announcements, they do not exist.

A gesture towards African Americans affects more than African American constituencies. It affects everyone who considers himself persecuted, disadvantaged, "underrepresented," or "oppressed." It affects just about everybody.

The principles I have outlined provide a guide for Republicans to avoid the mistakes of the past and to position the conservative cause as one that will free poor people and minorities from the oppressions of liberalism and the welfare state. A word remains to be said about the relation between principles and political tactics. Because politics is the art of the practical, it is often a complicated relationship and easily misunderstood.

POLITICS AND PRINCIPLES

No New Taxes

To make the point clearly, I will formulate it as provocatively as possible. The cornerstone of George Bush's 1988 election was his challenge to the voters to "read my lips: no new taxes." The act that caused George Bush to lose the 1992 election was the deal he made two years later with congressional Democrats to raise taxes. Conservative critics of George Bush say he lost because he was unprincipled. Here is my contrarian formulation: From a conservative point of view, the tax hike was morally sound, but politically stupid.

To understand this paradox, we need to go back to the context in which Bush signed the deal that broke his pledge. At the time, Democrats controlled the Congress and with it both the appropriations process and the ability to make war. Iraq's dictator, Saddam Hussein, had just invaded and conquered Kuwait and his armies were poised on the borders of an oil-rich and relatively defenseless Saudi Arabia. As an unpunished aggressor with the treasury of conquered Kuwait in his pocket, Saddam posed an imminent threat to the oil supplies of Europe and Asia. A Middle East war with Israel, possibly involving nuclear weapons, was a real prospect.

In this context, President Bush decided the national interest required him to stop the aggressor, by force if necessary. The Democratic Party, long adjusted to appeasing America's international enemies, opposed the use of force and insisted on negotiations even after negotiations had become an obvious charade. As commander in chief of the armed forces responsible for America's security, Bush decided he could not wage a two-front war—one against Saddam Hussein abroad and the other against the Democrats at home. He needed an appropriation for the war, knowing that Democrats would not cut domestic spending to pay for it. He needed Democrats' political support to gain authorization for the deployment itself.

This was the dilemma George Bush faced when he agreed to the Democrats' deal to raise taxes to underwrite the budget. This gave him the war funds he needed and the support of enough Democrats to authorize the war policy. Even with his concession, however, Bush only got the authorization to go to war by a hair. Only six Democratic senators voted to authorize the deployment of forces for Desert

Storm. The final vote was fifty-two to forty-seven. If three Democrats had voted the other way, the authorization would have failed.

Conservatives are against raising taxes, but conservatives also want to protect the United States and the free nations of the world from tyrannical predators like Saddam Hussein. Conservatives are also realists (or should be). In the crisis that led to the Gulf War, the Democrats had enough power in Congress to sabotage the war effort. Given the way the political battle had shaped up, Bush did not have the power to bring the Democrats to heel. Was the price of higher taxes worth the gain of stopping Saddam Hussein? That was the question George Bush faced. His answer was yes. Given the balance of political forces at that moment, what conservative could fault him for his decision?

But in taking the correct moral course, George Bush had made a political miscalculation that was fatal to his career. He had trusted Democrats to be honorable men who would not use his good faith and a deal they themselves had proposed to destroy his political career. His calculation was wrong. Once the Gulf War was over and won, the Democrats turned on their former ally. They ignored their own authorship of the tax hike and used it as a political weapon to destroy George Bush and elect Bill Clinton. The fact that Bush had made the pledge of "no new taxes" the centerpiece of his 1988 election campaign was enough to seal his fate.

The mistakes Bush made were entirely political. He thought he was dealing with people who were concerned about America's national interest and for whom partisanship died at the water's edge. He did not realize how far to the left the Democratic Party had swung and how treacherous its congressional leadership had become in the years following the Vietnam War. He did not realize the political danger he was in when he signed a deal he considered necessary to stop Saddam Hussein.

There were other political remedies available to George Bush, if he had had the political instincts to pursue them. He could have rejected the Democrats' deal and waged a public relations war against their appeasement politics. He could have attempted to shame them before the American people and forced them to support the effort on his terms by cutting domestic spending. This would have been a tough assignment and a risky one. If it had succeeded, Bush might have won the 1992 election. However, it was not in George Bush's political profile to conduct an aggressive political war like this.

Even after Desert Storm, with victory fresh in American minds, he might have saved his presidency by conducting an election campaign that punished the Democrats for their appeasement and explained the reasons he had to sign the tax deal. He could have waged a political war against the majority of Democrats who had opposed the Gulf War and had forced him to accept the budget compromise. He could have campaigned on the theme that the Democratic Party could not be trusted with the nation's security (although, to be fair, both Clinton and Gore supported the war).

Perhaps this kind of campaign would have saved his presidency. But, as a gracious man and a political moderate, George Bush chose not to take this course. It was this failure to nail his political enemies at home, to make them pay for their appeasement (not only of Iraq but of the Soviet Empire before it) that finally sank George Bush at the polls. His was a political failure, not a moral one.

We began this whole discussion with a question: Why do Republicans lose when they have a winning hand? This next case shows how politics can trump principle in local elections.

The Perils of Purism

The forty-first state assembly district in California extends from the liberal West side of Los Angeles through the more conservative municipalities of the San Fernando Valley. Currently, it has a registration that is 49 percent Democratic and 33 percent Republican, while 13 percent decline to state their affiliation. In 1996, this electorate voted 55 percent to 45 percent in favor of ending racial preferences, 70 percent to 30 percent for the three-strikes anticrime initiative, 54 percent to 47 percent for ending illegal immigration, and 59 percent to 41 percent against raising taxes on top-tier income voters. But in 1998 it voted 55 percent to 38 percent to elect Sheila Kuehl, a left-wing gay activist and a vocal advocate on the opposite side of all these issues.

How could this happen? It's the politics, stupid.

Kuehl is a former child actress who played Zelda on the television show *Dobie Gillis*. She won because she ran a slick campaign, successfully presenting herself as a "sensible Democrat," who was responsible and moderate, while her Republican opponent failed to define her as the leftist she actually was. Worse, she was able to project herself as caring and tolerant to a community that also voted 55 percent to 45 percent to raise the minimum wage, 64 percent to 36 percent to legalize marijuana for medical purposes, and 67 percent to 33 percent for a tobacco tax that would fund programs for pre-school children. Her opponent was a fairly typical Republican candidate, an honest businessman and a stand-up conservative. But the image he projected to the voters was that of a responsible accountant—fiscally cautious, socially rigid—a Republican without a heart. This image defeated him.

The voters in the forty-first assembly district did not share all conservatives' social values, but neither did they share all Sheila Kuehl's "liberal" values. Indeed, on at least three divisive and defining issues—racial preferences, illegal immigration, and class-warfare taxes—they were strongly opposed to Kuehl's views. Yet Kuehl won by a landslide. The result was that Sheila Kuehl went to Sacramento, where she worked to undermine the California Civil Rights Initative and the anti-illegal immigration law and to raise taxes. Sheila Kuehl knew how to conduct political warfare; her Republican opponent did not.

Politics is about winning elections and implementing programs. Because there is no majority in America that agrees on all the important issues, politics is about forming winning coalitions and holding them together. It is about getting people who disagree with each other to form an alliance. In short, it is about compromise. This does not mean that it is not also about principle. That is how you form your faction in the coalition and how you achieve anything once in office. If you are not willing to go to the mat for your core principles, you will lose your base and eventually lose the cause as well. The art of politics is to know how to get your principles implemented without compromising them too much.

Conservative Republicans often condemn compromise without making distinctions, but their hero, Ronald Reagan, was a famous compromiser. Throughout his administration he allowed deficits that no conservative could justify in good conscience. He did so because his choices were limited by political realities. The Democratic spenders controlled the Congress and the government's purse strings. They opposed increases in the military budget and were inclined to appease the communists during a dangerous Cold War. Ronald Reagan was a political visionary. He wanted to defeat the "evil empire" and free the economy from the chains of big government. But what made him the most successful president in the last forty years was that he focused on what was important to him and did not let the purists dissuade him from his mission.

Reagan's priorities were tax cuts and winning the Cold War. He gave the Democrats their spending programs in order to get them to agree to a radical reduction in marginal tax rates and a dramatic increase in the military budget. He gave one negative (deficits) to get two positives (prosperity and peace). He compromised principle, but for a greater good.

The problem of political purism is always with us. The reason for this is that many people confuse politics and religion. Politics is the art of the possible; religion is the pursuit of an ideal. Religion is about getting into heaven; politics is about getting into office. In religious matters, integrity of principle is not only an advantage, it is the goal itself. Religion is not about getting tax cuts or building schools; it is about saving souls. Being virtuous and right, having integrity and standing on principle, are its very essence. You cannot compromise with the devil and expect to get to heaven. In politics, on the other hand, pacts with the devil are made all the time. This can even be regarded as a healthy development. The twentieth century is littered with the corpses of people who got in the way of uncompromising zealots—Hitler, Lenin, Pol Pot—who thought they were on a religious mission of social redemption. The appropriate places for making people moral and good are churches and synagogues and mosques, not state houses or congressional hearing rooms.

Many conservatives do not want to face the real world problems that their purist attitudes create. They want to have it both ways. They think that by being morally correct conservatives can win. In fact, they think that is the only way Republicans can win. The Republican problem, they say, is not an inability to understand political tactics. The Republican problem is "lack of backbone," by which they mean the failure to stand up for conservative principles. Political timidity is certainly a Republican problem, and being on the defensive generally means losing the political war. But is this defensiveness the result of a lack of principle, or is it a lack of confidence in facing the enemy? In my view, Republicans blink not because they lack principle, but because they are convinced the firepower of the left is superior to their own.

The blinking does not come from the kind of soft-headed politics associated with the moderates who once ran the Republican Party. Today's Republican Party is a long way from the party of Nelson Rockefeller or even Bob Michel. If the current House Republicans were mainly spineless, there would have been no "Contract With America." The House Republicans became squishy after the "train wreck" of 1995, when they were outmaneuvered by the White House. Only two years later, however, they showed they could still stand up for principle when they impeached the president, even though the polls were against them and they failed to remove him.

The House Republicans disregarded Clinton's 70 percent poll ratings because they were committed to defend the constitutional process. Yet they could hardly ignore that Clinton survived their assault. Clinton was able to survive a year that no other politician could have survived because of his mastery of political combat. Beholding Clinton's bulletproof persona naturally made Republicans cautious. The Republicans' problem is that they are psychologically beaten in advance by an opponent who knows how to fight better. This has nothing to do with Republicans being compromisers or cowards. The same men who led the Class of 1994 and won the famous victories are the men who ordered the retreat.

Look at Clinton and ask yourself: How does he do it? How does he commit adultery in the White House, perjure himself before a grand jury, lie to the American people, and yet prevail in political combat all at the same time?

The answer is the children. The answer is the blacks. The answer is the poor. It is the Democratic version of wrapping yourself in the American flag. Like every successful Democrat, Clinton wraps himself in the flag of the "dispossessed." He says: "However badly you think of me, I'm all that stands between women, children, minorities, and the poor and those hard-hearted Republicans, who are closet racists as well." Until the Republican Party takes this weapon out of the Democratic arsenal, Republicans are doomed to long-term frustration and defeat. In marginal districts and at the national level Republicans can win only when Democrats betray their leftist beliefs. But if Republicans can learn to fight the way Democrats do, they might well become the majority party, as their policies merit.

This prescription for success can be summarized using the "triangulation" terminology invented by Clinton's Republican pollster Dick Morris. To convince American voters that Democrats could be fiscally responsible and socially tough-minded, Clinton triangulated with Republicans by appropriating Republican policies that reflected those values. Republicans need to reverse the process and triangulate with the rhetoric of Democrats that has proven mass appeal. (Needless to say, not all rhetoric is fungible. The Democrats' class-warfare and race-baiting appeals are contrary to Republican principles and to the interests of the public good, and would be counterproductive if adopted.) Remember: It's about convincing the ordinary citizen that your policies flow from concern for them—and from fear of your opponents' agendas.

DEMOCRATS AND REPUBLICANS

Republicans are not a party parallel to Democrats or separated only by different views of certain issues. During presidential elections the two parties often converge on the center, suggesting to ideologues and the casually observant that they are peas in a pod. But this is only a seasonal illusion. The reality is that Democrats and Republicans differ not only over principles and policies; they are different political breeds.

Democrats come to party politics out of socialist organizations, trade unions, and an assortment of social crusades (abortion, racial grievances, and environmental concerns). They are combat-ready before they begin their political careers. Republicans train in Boy Scout troops and graduate to chambers of commerce and rotary clubs. Except for the pro-life missionaries in the conservative coalition, Republicans are innocents abroad when it comes to political war.

Democrats and Republicans also have different reasons for entering politics. Republicans want to manage institutions; Democrats seek to transform them. Republicans go to Washington with the idea of fixing government; Democrats are on a mission to fix the world. Because of its inspiration, the Republican agenda is largely negative. Republicans want to shrink government, reduce its tax base, and cut regulations. When they try to enact more radical agendas (eliminating public television and the Department of Education), their moderate constituencies desert them, and they lose. Even when Republicans want to increase spending on a government program like the military, there is a negative motive behind their actions—they want to end a threat, not start something new.

Democrats are missionaries. They want to make the world "a better place" (and not by getting government off people's backs). Even their negatives spring from a positive ambition: to create a better brand of human being, to save people from themselves. They regard themselves and government as social redeemers. If Americans have bad thoughts, Democrats want to use political power to reeducate citizens in diversity seminars and sensitivity training sessions to make their thoughts good. If Americans have bad habits, Democrats want government to punish them until they change. They want to use the power of the tax system to make Americans stop smoking or stop driving gas-guzzling automobiles. Above all, they want to stop Americans from spending their money on themselves and their families, and instead give it to others who Democrats think are more deserving. By contrast, the conservative attitude is that in trying to change the world the left can (and usually does) make things worse.

Because the stakes (saving—or at least uplifting—the world) are so high for Democrats, it matters a great deal to them if they lose elections. On the other hand, with the threat of communism gone from the post-Cold War world, Republicans often behave as if they could not care less. If Republican candidates do not win, they can always go back to business and enjoy life. Republicans do not care that much about politics because the stakes are usually so low. The private sector is still a big, opportunity-rich arena. Fixing government is no big deal.

A model of the Democratic activist is provided by the life and tragic death of Helen Bernstein who was once head of the teachers' union and a candidate for local office in Los Angeles. Helen Bernstein was fifty-two years old and the mother of a seventeen-year-old daughter when she decided to run for one of the fifteen Los Angeles City Council seats—thirteen of which were already held by Democrats in a city that is Democratic heaven. An evening came during the campaign when Bernstein realized she was late for one of the interminable little meetings with the public that every local candidate endures. Arms loaded with literature and campaign flyers, she ran across Wilshire Boulevard to get to her meeting and was hit by oncoming traffic. Thus ended a dedicated life.

What was so important to Helen Bernstein that it was worth her life? The answer to that question holds the secret of the Democrats' political success. For missionaries like Helen Bernstein, the cause—changing the world—is so great that every election counts. To lose a seat even in a minor election is a setback in the struggle for a better world. I do not know of any Republicans killed in the line of duty like Helen Bernstein.

While not every Democratic activist is so driven, every issue that Democrats contest is colored in their minds by the larger purpose of redeeming the world through government. Because of the nobility of their intentions, they are able to make their failures seem like successes and are able to convince others of this too. A *New York Times*-CBS poll at the end of 1999 showed, for example, that "Democrats enjoy public confidence on most critical election issues, from health care to education to Social Security." Is that because Democrats have done so well managing healthcare, education, and welfare? According to Democrats themselves, every one of these systems was in crisis at the time the poll was taken, and every one of them required billions of additional dollars to repair.

Some of the "crises" were more rhetorical than real, but others—like the crisis in education—were not. Shortly after the poll was published, the *Los Angeles Times* reported that a plan to end "social promotion" in the city's schools and to hold back children who had not passed their grades had to be scrapped. The reason administrators gave was that they had conducted an investigation and concluded that they would have to hold back 350,000 children—*half of the entire school system*—because they had failed to learn the required work and would be forced to repeat the school year under the plan. This is not a "crisis." This is a social catastrophe, engulfing hundreds of thousands of mostly poor, mostly Hispanic and African American children in Los Angeles' public schools who are being systematically deprived of the opportunity to change their lives. Helen Bernstein and her Democratic and teacher union friends are responsible for this—but no one thinks to blame them. Among politicians, evading responsibility is practically an art form, making it sometimes difficult to tell who is responsible for which governmental mess. But in areas like education policy, it is not too hard to see who are the sheep and who the goats.

Education is not principally a federal issue. More than 90 percent of education dollars are raised and spent at the local level. Hence, the national Republican administrations of previous decades can hardly be held responsible for this disaster. Nor can the two Republican congresses of the last forty years. In most major urban areas, there is a hardly a single elected Republican on any school board or in charge of administering any district. Democrats, liberals, and not a few marxists have controlled most of the big-city school systems in America for the last sixty years, including those in the big metropolitan districts: New York, Chicago, Los Angeles, Baltimore, Boston, and Washington, D.C. The bottom line is that Democrats are responsible for everything that has gone wrong with the public schools that can be caused or fixed by public policies.

Yet Democrats have the public's confidence on education, which is perceived as a "Democratic issue." How can this be? Is it because the Democratic slander—that Republicans do not care about education—has some bite to it? Is it because even though Republicans do care, they do not have an answer to the failures that Democratic policies have produced? Is it because they do not have programs to rescue poor and minority children from the fate to which Democrats have consigned them? In fact, Republicans do care and do have solutions. What they do not have is the foggiest idea of how to present these programs to the American electorate in a way that would win its confidence. They do not have a clue as to how to fight the political battle.

While politics is war conducted by other means, Republicans are often reluctant to fire a shot. They may oppose trigger locks for real guns, but they are willing to put their political guns in lock boxes and throw away the keys. In the debate over schools during the 1999 budget negotiation, for example, Republicans more or less withdrew from the contest and allowed Democrats to position themselves as the education party. During the maneuvering over the budget, the Democrats were able (as usual) to position themselves as champions of children and the Republicans as education scrooges. The Republican response to the Democrats' proposals was the usual wimp-out: "Okay, we'll concede some of the money you're asking for the same old programs, just to show we're not really as hard-hearted as you say. We'll let the president have the funding he wants for one hundred thousand new teachers and call it a 'solution,' even though we have our doubts it will work, since the teachers will still be paid not for producing results but just for showing up. The president is really just kicking tax dollars back to the unions that support him."

What the public hears of this congressional debate is the same old sound bite: Democrats want more money for education; Republicans want less. Any deeper analysis is lost in the static. If Republicans are lucky, the public will hear that Republicans may care about education, but not as much as Democrats. Electorally, it does not make a big difference. Of course, many voters are already not listening to Republicans because the Democrats have convinced them that all Republicans care about are "tax breaks for the rich."

If the education crisis could be solved by adding more teachers to the payrolls, who would be opposed to that? The problem is that Democrats have been adding teachers and funds for decades, but the education crisis has only gotten worse. Republicans have an explanation: You can add all the teachers and funds you want, but if there is no connection between teachers' performance and their rewards, there will be no improvement. Without some competition, no education plan will work. One may disagree whether "vouchers" or "opportunity scholarships" or a drastic weakening of the union lobby is the way to connect educational performance and reward, but there is no doubt that the Democratic Party, tied as it is to bankrupt policies and union interests, is the party least likely to deliver a result.

How can Republicans get their message to the electorate? Only by doing what Democrats do. First, they can attack their opponents' credibility. As long as the public believes that Democrats are the party to trust when it comes to education, Republican arguments will fall on deaf ears. Here is a message Republicans could use to neutralize the confidence the public mistakenly places in Democrats: "Democrats have crippled and nearly destroyed the public education system through fifty years of bureaucratic bungling and selfish policies that benefit the unions. In major cities, the public schools are failing to graduate nearly 50 percent of their minority students. Lack of education usually leads to a lifetime of poverty. In the past, public schools were the path to success for America's immigrants and poor. Now they are dead ends for kids with no future. No Democrat in Congress sends his or her own children to public schools. Why should they be allowed to condemn the children of minorities and the poor to a failed system to whom they wouldn't entrust their own children? It's time to end this social tragedy, to give these kids a shot at the American dream."

This is the message, but where is the Republican who will give it? If Republicans do not identify Democrats as the cause of the education crisis *going in* to the policy debate, they have already tied one hand behind their backs, cupped the other over their mouths, and put hundred-pound weights around their legs. As a result of Republicans' ineptitude at political war, Democrats have become a "teflon" party, able to escape the social disasters their policies create.

MAKING THEIR CASE

This noncombatant attitude is so pervasive in Republican politics that it even affects their ability to hold their ground in territory that is traditionally theirs. Consider the "Republican issue" of national defense. For the last fifty years, American voters have (correctly) trusted Republicans to defend the national interest better than Democrats, who have appeared "soft" on America's adversaries in international affairs and unwilling to spend the necessary dollars on the military. But consider the political fallout when Republicans rejected the Clinton-sponsored Comprehensive Test Ban Treaty in the winter of 1999.

The Senate debate pitted the parties' philosophies against each other. Democrats favored an arms control agreement because, as liberals, they believe in the fundamental good intentions of most human beings and their ability to use reason in their own interest. Republicans opposed the treaty because they are skeptical of arms control strategies and suspicious of good intentions. Democrats defended the nuclear test ban treaty as a moment of truth for American leadership. Ratification, they argued, would set an example to other nations to pursue a path of sanity and restraint. Rejecting the treaty would be to abandon America's leadership role, leaving the world to its own devices. Republicans had a different idea. They argued that arms control programs have failed over the years and are dangerous precisely because of that fact.

The international arms control policies implemented after World War I are a good example. Western democracies—America, England and France—observed the treaties, but the dictatorships—Germany and Japan—did not. Arms control illusions allowed the Axis powers to gain a military advantage in the interwar years and tempted them to risk a military confrontation. These illusions were a major cause (some would say *the* major cause) of World War II. During the Cold War, the United States again observed arms control agreements, but its opponents did not. Arms control tied America's hands but not its adversaries'. Republicans saw no reason to believe that the new treaty would be any different in practice.

The Comprehensive Test Ban Treaty was a moment of truth for both parties. Republicans had a better sense of history and a better view of human nature supporting their arguments. They opposed the Comprehensive Test Ban Treaty because existing technologies could not verify whether small nuclear explosions had actually taken place. Such tests were necessary to the development of nuclear weapons by powers like China, Iraq, and other despotic states, but there was no way to ensure that they would forgo the tests and observe the treaty once they had signed it. China supported the treaty, since China's dictators knew that it would tie America's hands but not their own. The United States, which has an open society, would be compelled to observe the treaty's terms. Closed societies like China and its allies, Iran, Libya, and Iraq, would not.

Republicans had the better side of the argument. Both history and realism dictated that the United States should not sign. In the end, their majority enabled them to kill the treaty, yet they lost the public debate. The reason was that while Democrats lost the congressional vote, they immediately went on the political offensive. The Senate's rejection of the treaty was accompanied by White House charges that Republicans were "isolationists," unwilling to face the realities of the modern world. Prior to the Cold War, isolationism had a powerful hold on Republican sensibilities. Republican isolationists believed that if America retreated to its continental fortress, it could ignore what happened in the world outside.

But that was more than fifty years ago, when the Republican Party was a very different coalition than it is now. Republicans abandoned their isolationist positions in 1948, when their leading spokesman, Senator Arthur Vandenburg, announced his support for the Truman Doctrine and the Cold War against the Soviet empire. Republicans stayed the course, maintaining the Cold War internationalism of the Truman Administration until the Berlin Wall finally fell. To accuse Republicans of being an isolationist party given this history, was a bold political lie.

That did not stop Clinton, of course. But while a liberal media supported this partisan assault, Republicans were slack-jawed, politically paralyzed. Instead of launching a counter-attack, they scrambled for public microphones to explain that they had been misunderstood. It was untrue that they were isolationists and unfair to label them so. The sound bites the public heard were: Republicans are isolationists; Republicans deny the charge. It does not take a Dick Morris to figure out which position has the advantage.

What the voting public failed to hear was any charge against the Democratic opponents of the treaty. There was no label like "isolationist" to stick to the other side. One such label Republicans could have used for their Democratic opponents was "appeasers," since Clinton had already revived the terms of the prewar debate. The Test Ban Treaty was about appeasing regimes like China's, a ruthless dictatorship that has never signed an agreement it was not prepared to break. Applying the "appeaser" charge to the President would have underscored the fact that the Comprehensive Test Ban Treaty was in part designed to mollify dictatorships, potential aggressors, and generally notorious violators of international norms. It would have reminded voters that, once again, Democrats had let their liberal optimism fog their political vision.

I made this suggestion to the communications director of the Republican National Committee, and I received the following reply: "Republicans did not label the Democrats appeasers in the test-ban debate, because Trent Lott does not believe that Bill Clinton is an appeaser."

My response was this: "First, Bill Clinton *is* an appeaser. Second, this is politics! Do you think Bill Clinton really believes that Republicans are isolationists? He's tagged you with a big negative and you haven't tagged him back. Wake up. You've lost! Do you think voters are going to give Republicans a gold star for meticulous use of language, accuracy, and good behavior?"

A far more troubling zone of Republican ineptitude is race. Here, Democrats are able to play their trump cards with ease. Republicans are so regularly and so roundly beaten on the race issue, Democrats merely have to show up in order to win. In the winter of 1999, all Democrats had to do was nominate a corrupt and morally challenged African American for an ambassadorial position in order to create a boobytrap for Republicans. If Republicans ratified the nomination of former Senator Carol Moseley-Braun, Democrats would win the acclaim of the African American community. If Republicans opposed her nomination, Democrats could insinuate they were racists. In both cases, Democrats could count on Republicans to cooperate in their own defeat.

As a senator, Carol Moseley-Braun was notorious for defying the policy of her own government and cozying up to Nigeria's dictator—a sadistic oppressor of black Africans. In doing so, Moseley-Braun had brought on herself the ire of the Clinton Administration and even left-wing organizations like Randall Robinson's TransAfrica. Did Republicans remind Democrats of this when her nomination came up? Did they point to her lack of concern for suffering Nigerians and her ethical lapses in office which made her nomination an insult to all Americans and to African Americans in particular?

Instead, the Republicans' senatorial champion Jesse Helms made it clear that his motive in opposing her nomination was revenge for a stance she had taken against the confederate flag! *The night they drove old Dixie down, all the liberals were singing. . . .*

Shortly after this episode, I arrived in Bloomfield Hills, a prosperous suburb of Detroit, to speak to Republican activists. The campaign manager for the local Republican congressman picked me up at the airport. During the trip, I asked him the following question about the 2000 election, at the time exactly a year away: "The economy is booming and people have money in their pockets. Give me three reasons why anyone should vote for a Republican this year?"

The silence was long and painful. Another party activist, who was along for the ride, intervened to offer a laborious explanation of why he felt Republicans' philosophy of limited government and respect for the individual meant that Republican politicians could be better entrusted with the power of the state than Democrats. His argument dragged on for a few minutes before I interrupted him.

"Look," I said. "There's going to be an election in twelve months. It's probably the most important election in twenty years. Voters who trust Republicans already vote Republican. You have less than thirty seconds to reach the average undecided voter who, by the way, is completely uninterested in the political process, and thinks all politicians are interchangeable, not to mention low on the scale of beings you can put your trust in. What are you going to say to them to get *their* vote?"

Silence.

"I'll give you some help. Democrats have already hunkered down in their war rooms. They already know their 'line of march.' They've identified the issues they believe will sink you and have the sound bites ready to go. It's no mystery, because they're out there with them already. They're going to run on the environment, abortion, and gun control for starters. Here's how: 'If you elect Republicans, they'll give the corporate polluters a field day and take away the air you breathe. If you elect Republicans, they'll invite the government into your bedroom to tell your wife or daughter what to do with her pregnancy and therefore with the rest of her life. If you elect Republicans, they'll make guns available to disturbed children, turn them into serial killers and let them loose in your children's schools.'"

I paused, to wait for a response. None came. "Take a look at how those propositions are formulated," I continued. "They are war cries. They give people a life-and-death reason to vote. They make Republicans appear to be the enemies of children, women, and all humanity. They show that Democrats care about their safety and well-being. They take ten seconds to get across. What is your response?"

The Republican campaign manager and the Republican activist just sat there.

This, in a nutshell, is the Republican problem. Republicans are problem-solvers not ideological warriors. They are not prepared for the political battle the Democrats have come to fight. This is more than just a partisan dilemma. It is a national tragedy. Translated into human terms, the success of modern Democratic Party liberalism has meant millions of blighted lives in America's inner cities, an unconscionable tax burden on America's middle classes, and an unsafe living environment for us all. This is reason enough to support the Republican agenda. If only Republicans knew how to make their case.

II

Modern Savonarolas

I

When Liberals Censor . . .

SOME YEARS AGO, I attended an event in Nashville sponsored by
Vice President Al Gore. It was one of Gore's annual "family
reunions," a gathering of liberal media experts whose purpose
was to provide a scientific rationale for the censorship that he and
President Clinton, who also attended, were preparing to launch
against the nation's entertainment industry. The event was held in
an auditorium at Vanderbilt University, and Gore directed the conversation from the stage. With all the obtuseness that seems hard-
wired into his thought process, the vice president several times
repeated the following proposition: "It seems obvious to me that the
link between real-world violence and television violence is exactly
analogous to the link between cigarette smoking and cancer." Of the
two hundred "experts" attending the event, only Jack Valenti, Tom
Selleck, and I dissented, and only we spoke out against the "v-chip"
that Clinton and Gore were unveiling that day.

When Gore singled me out to speak, I asked the following questions: If television is responsible for real-world violence, why are crime
rates so different in various neighborhoods of a given city, when the

television shows are the same? How could those attending this event have witnessed one hundred thousand murders on television, as the academic experts had solemnly informed us we had, without becoming desensitized and violence-prone, as the same experts had claimed a television-watcher would? From the back of the auditorium, Jack Valenti held up a list of the sixty Nielsen top-rated network television shows and observed that "not a single one of them is violent." He might as well have been speaking to the deaf.

A summary moment came when Betty Friedan, icon to virtually all the liberals present, rose to her feet and said that though she believed in the First Amendment, she was glad to see that the left and right had finally agreed on something: the need for censorship of television programming. She hoped the vice president would not be intimidated by those who would tell him that government should not play an active role in making society a better place. Then it was my turn, and though I sensed the audience was growing increasingly hostile to my point of view, I responded: "What Betty Friedan just said sent chills up my spine." Before I could get any farther, there was an eruption in the first row, where the vice president's wife, Tipper, was sitting. Racing up the aisle to where I was sitting, Mrs. Gore sputtered in my face words to the effect that I was a liar and worse. I had insulted a feminist legend; what Friedan really wanted was a better world.

It was an incident that turned my apolitical bride-to-be into a Republican on the spot, so dismayed was she by the spectacle. Perhaps liberals' rudeness—which seems a second nature—is reason enough to become a Republican. But the puritan impulse to censor and control others seems to be bipartisan.

The v-chip, it needs to be said, is a crude device that will not help children whose parents are already derelict or absent (in other words, those who need it most). Moreover, it is dangerous to the most precious freedom Americans' have. Al Gore, who has been an outspoken champion of parental boycotts of offending television shows, points out that if 3 percent of parents use the v-chip to block a particular show "advertisers will go elsewhere." Since it is entirely conceivable that 3 percent of parents might object to a quality show with violence, like *Roots*—which detailed the history of African Americans' odyssey through slavery in this country—it is also possible that such shows would not be made. This is the little problem that zealots like Gore and Friedan choose to ignore.

While almost all Democrats in Congress supported the v-chip legislation, most Republicans opposed it when the White House team first floated the idea. Philosophically, Republicans are averse to regulation and are committed to the idea of individual responsibility in making such choices. Viewers can turn off the television to avoid programming they do not like. Even Ralph Reed, then head of the Christian Coalition, and the Reverend Donald Wildmon, leader of a boycott of *The Last Temptation of Christ*, opposed the v-chip on the grounds that government was taking over a family responsibility.

It was only by striking a devil's pact in the eleventh hour with a rump group of Republicans from the Christian Right that Massachussetts Democrat Edward Markey was able to sneak the v-chip into the 1996 Telecommunications Bill. Fifteen or so votes made the difference. But once the v-chip was law and the Clinton White House showed how politically popular censorship could be, Republicans began to pile on.

The watershed was probably Clinton's post–v-chip state of the union address, when he summoned the heads of all the media giants to the White House to face the music. In his speech he had looked into the cameras and told the entertainment industry he wanted it to make films and television shows that its leaders would be proud to show their grandchildren. No one commented afterwards how absurd the request was. Was he proposing that the nation's film fare to be reduced to the level of Bambi and the Muppets?

Nor was there an editorial outcry across the nation condemning the outrage the president had committed against the Fourth Estate. The executive branch of government, after all, wields life-and-death power over the media industry through its control of the broadcast spectrum and regulatory agencies. The precedent Bill Clinton set that day will haunt Americans for a long time to come.

Liberals kept silent because Clinton is one of them and they did not want to upset his applecart. Conservatives like John McCain, the powerful head of the Commerce Committee in charge of all tele-communications legislation, saw a political opportunity and joined the charge.

Liberals and conservatives have different demons they want to exorcise, which creates the illusion that their instincts for censorship are different. For liberals it is violence that offends; for conservatives it is sex. In 1999, in the wake of a series of shootings on high school campuses, Judiciary Committee chairman Henry Hyde thought he had a found a way to split the difference by defining violence as "obscene" and making it a criminal offense to purvey "obscene violent images" to children. Though Hyde's attempt mercifully failed, it had support across the left-right spectrum, including Republican moderates like Christopher Shays, Sherwood Boehlert, and Jim Greenwood, as well as conservatives like Helen Chenoweth and Steve Largent.

Violent obscenity was defined in the Hyde Amendment as a "visual depiction of an actual or simulated display of, or a detailed verbal description or narrative account of a sadistic or masochistic flagellation by or upon a person, torture by or upon a person, acts of mutilation of the human body, or rape." Lawyers for the Interdigital Software Association (makers of video games) pointed out that, under this definition, the whipping of the slave Kunte Kinte in *Roots* would qualify as obscene and would send its makers to jail if the video was marketed to minors. They also wondered whether the law would apply to violent acts committed on animated characters.

This would bring into the net the feature film *South Park* , which provided the first irreverent and irresistible opposition to the tide of censorship sweeping both parties. Cultural reactionaries were in various stages of apoplexy over the moon-faced midgets' television show, whose political incorrectness was already a cult obsession. According to a (conservative) Focus on the Family publication, *South Park* is a "twisted new series about a group of foul-mouthed third-graders." It warned that "the spoiled chubby kid responds to taunts with shouts of 'go to hell' and 'screw you.'" An Associated Press story indicated how broad the potential backlash was: "Denise Clapham, a mother of four from Brunswick, NY, [is] not thrilled that her 16-year-old son and his friends are fans." Said Clapham of the show: "I think they can be funny without being that far out, and I'm a liberal."

Peggy Charen, the most celebrated liberal advocate of a government mandated "children's television hour" faulted the show's tone and the words that the characters throw around. "It's the words they use in ordinary life, in the cafeteria, in the school room, that's dangerous to the democracy," according to Charen. My own guess is that what Peggy Charen really did not like was the send-up of the sensitivity crowd that has made her their hero. In a famous episode of the *South Park* television series, entitled "Damien," a new kid enters the class:

Teacher: Now some of you know what it's like to be the new kid in
town, so I want you all to take special care to make him feel
welcome. I want you all to meet our new classmate . . . uh,
what's your name again?

Damien: Damien!

[Weird Latinate chanting begins. There are flames in Damien's eyes.]

Teacher: Say hi to Damien!

[Silence]

Teacher: And where are you from Damien?

Damien: The seventh layer of Hell!

Teacher: Oh, that's exciting. My mother was from Alabama.

[Weird chanting ensues.]

Damien: My arrival denotes the end of the beginning, the beginning
of the end. The new reign of my father!

Teacher: Your father?

Damien: The Prince of Darkness.

Teacher: Wow, we have royalty in our class.

It is not hard to see how literalists might have difficulty with these
scripts, but is that a reason to bring the eight-hundred-pound go-
rilla of government into the picture?

   In the midst of public concern over the shootings at Columbine
High School in Littleton, Colorado, I was paired with film critic
Michael Medved on Fox televisions' *O'Reilly Factor* to talk about new
film releases. Medved described the South Park movie as depraved
and not fit for mainstream release. It is "anti-kid and anti-God," he
commented. He is right that one of the South Park kids curses God.
But the kid explains, when asked, that he hates God because his
mother tried to abort him with a coat-hanger. You might think a
pro-life conservative like Medved would appreciate the satiric dis-
sonance. Unfortunately, irony seems out of reach for the Truly Seri-

ous. *South Park* is an "r-rated" film, requiring photo identification (and a paid ticket) for entry. So why should anybody have a problem with it, let alone a conservative?

The film is an acid commentary on efforts to have government put the genie of freedom into the bottle of political correctness. As the story unfolds, the South Park kids try to sneak into an r-rated film, featuring the foul-mouthed gas-passing Canadian comics Terrance and Philip. They succeed by giving a homeless derelict ten dollars to escort them in. The film makes an extreme impression on the kids, one of whom remarks that it "has warped my fragile little mind." They exit the theater speaking streams of expletives like Terrance and Philip.

The response of the South Park adults to the crisis that ensues— the kids take their foul-mouthed expressions first to school and then home—is just a comic extension of familiar attitudes. One of the South Park kids, named Cartman, is taken to a doctor who implants a v-chip in his head so that every time he curses he will get a shock. The parents of the delinquent kids refuse to take responsibility for their children's behavior and blame Canada for producing Terrance and Philip. An organization called Mothers Against Canada is formed to protest the foreign threat. Soon the scapegoating of Canada has escalated into a full-scale war.

Eventually it's the kids, of course, who restore sanity and peace. During a lightning storm, occasioned by the appearance of Satan and Saddam Hussein, the v-chip in Cartman's head is recircuited so that it becomes a weapon he can use to defeat the marauding adult armies. Every time Cartman uses a four-letter word, a bolt fires from his head and zaps its target. With this weapon, the children are able to defeat the forces of adult darkness that have engulfed their innocent—if foul-mouthed—world.

Unfortunately, in the real world, the book burners continue with their crusade. The Clinton team has already laid down clear markers in their assaults on the tobacco and gun industries. With government studies now authorized for an examination of the entertainment industry and with "scientific studies" to follow, it is not hard to visualize the lawsuits ahead. What makes these developments truly ominous is that the Republican opposition has all but caved. In the past, Republicans were defenders of the principle that lawful industries should not be destroyed by government lawsuit. But having defended tobacco—an industry that actually kills people—Republicans seem to be joining the lynch mob now that the target is a Democratic haven, albeit an industry that has killed no one.

The threat to films like *South Park* is a threat to all artistic expression. Milan Kundera wrote a classic novel about totalitarianism called *The Book of Laughter and Forgetting*. The point that Kundera was making about laughter was that it was absolutely subversive of totalitarian ideology, which invites citizens into circles of harmony and ends up binding them in chains of repression. In America, these chains are not so heavy yet, but because they are being forged by a bipartisan coalition, the danger should not be taken lightly.

2

. . . And Conservatives Follow

"IF LIBERALS CAN GET AWAY WITH IT, it must be all right," seems to be the latest conservative substitute for serious thinking. The left's latest crusade against "media pollution" has become a movement the right apparently cannot wait to join.

For some time now, conservatives have watched anxiously as tenured leftists have conducted mind experiments on American campuses, regulating speech and punishing ideas that are politically incorrect. Conservatives have even fought a rearguard battle against these academic commissars, managing to achieve a modicum of success. Most of the speech codes have been shredded, and the censors have been forced to beat a partial retreat. But the political mindset has remained, and its attitudes continue to rule the academic roost, which is always on guard against conservative heresies. As a result, no institution in American life is as intellectually monolithic as a university campus. Not unexpectedly, academic scholars on the left have provided an elaborate theory, and underpinned it with "scientific" research, to justify the resurgence of censorship in American life.

On the political right, religious conservatives have traditionally been attracted to antidemocratic fixes for sinful humanity. But now, even the secular minds of the conservative intelligentsia are being seduced. Even while they were being banished from American classrooms by their "liberal" betters, a cadre of conservative intellectuals was making the case for public censors. Arguing that artistic expressions are not covered by the Bill of Rights, they made government-funded pornographic art the first target of their complaint, while suggesting that even nongovernment licentiousness is also a proper government concern. When liberals like Bill Clinton and Tipper Gore showed that a puritan crusade against the media culture might actually become a popular cause, conservatives were eager to sign on.

Not long ago, both groups came together behind an "Appeal to Hollywood," complaining about the moral pollution of the popular culture. Mindful of Americans' quaint attachment to their First Amendment privileges, the "Appeal" only asked the entertainment industry to "take modest steps of self-restraint" to decrease the levels of sex and violence perceived in its products. The "Appeal" was signed by sixty-seven prominent public figures, members of a new popular front that joined such unlikely couples as Bill Bennett and Mario Cuomo, Jimmy Carter and Lynne Cheney.

But the "Appeal to Hollywood" is only part of a growing trend on both ends of the political spectrum to weaken the bulwarks that protect our First Amendment freedoms. Even as the "Appeal" was being released, the federal government was putting the entertainment industry on the block, slating it for investigation and restrictive legislation (to be followed, if precedent was any guide, by class-action lawsuits). The measures against Hollywood were consciously designed to parallel the ongoing assaults against manufacturers of cigarettes and guns. Considering that entertainment products are ideas, images, and fantasies, the mere linking of the three industries in this way should send shivers up the national spine.

Even this juggernaut of repression, however, did not seem enough for the editors of the conservative *Weekly Standard*, who devoted an issue to "The Case For Censorship," the title of a cover feature written by political scientist David Lowenthal.* The editors also invited four distinguished conservative intellectuals—Bill Bennett, Irving Kristol, Terry Eastland, and Jeremy Rabkin—to contribute their comments.

Lowenthal's manifesto was a screed in behalf of full-blown moral dictatorship by government guardians over what the public should see and hear. According to Lowenthal, Hollywood is so "enamored of its profits" that no appeals to its conscience would work. On the other hand, without drastic measures to stop the current flow of cultural filth, prospects for the nation were truly dire.

"The mass media," Lowenthal wrote, have become "the prime educational force in the country," and their "pernicious" influence already overwhelms that of "schools, synagogues and churches." They have "immersed us" in violence as well as sexual depravity, "habituated us to the most extreme brutality," and "surrounded us by images of hateful human types so memorable as to cause a psychological insecurity that is dangerous." Nothing less than the future of civilization is at stake and no power short of the state is sufficient to save us: "Government, and government alone, has a chance of blocking this descent into decadence. . . . The choice is clear: either a rigorous censorship of the mass media . . . or an accelerating descent into barbarism and the destruction, sooner or later of free society itself."

---

* David Lowenthal, "The Case for Censorship," *Weekly Standard* 4:46 (August 23, 1999): 21-24. See also David Lowenthal, *No Liberty for License: The Forgotten Logic of the First Amendment* (Dallas: Spence Publishing, 1997), especially chapter ten.

Even more distressing than this jeremiad was the failure of any of the conservative commentators assembled by the *Standard* to find it distressing. "I agree with much in Professor Lowenthal's article," wrote Bill Bennett, while describing himself as a "First Amendment absolutist." But how absolute could Bennett's commitment to the First Amendment be if he did not condemn Lowenthal's proposal? Instead of rejecting it as an antidemocratic manifesto, Bennett criticized its political imprudence. The "main problem for Lowenthal's argument," he wrote, "is democracy itself, specifically the current state of thinking among the American people: They do not want, to use Lowenthal's words, 'rigorous censorship.'"

And if they did, would that be all right?

What Bennett proposed, instead, was an effort to bring the industry to heel by a combination of public humiliation and government threats. "Among other things, Congress ought to begin treating the entertainment industry the same way it treats the gun and tobacco industries: Invite the executives to testify in public, let them defend [themselves]. . . . Is there *anything* you won't sell? Why was this ugly, stupid, horrible scene put in this movie?"

So now congressmen are going to be theater critics. I wonder if Bennett has thought about the scene that would have takent place if the English Parliament had hauled Shakespeare before it, in the time of Elizabeth, to explain why both eyes of the eighty-year-old Duke of Gloucester are plucked out on stage in *King Lear*, or a virginal Ophelia has such obscene fantasies in *Hamlet* or why eight people are killed in the last scene of the same play. "Mr. Shakespeare! Is this *really* necessary? Don't you find eight corpses a little excessive? Have you no *shame*, sir?"

The contribution of lawyer and *American Spectator* publisher Terry Eastland was even less restrained than Bennett's. "Censor the mass media? In theory, I agree," he began. But then he, too, was forced to concede the practical objections to such a plan. There is the tricky matter, for example, of American law which "stands in the way" of the kind of censorship Lowenthal proposed, particularly as it has been interpreted for the last fifty years. Behind current interpretations of the law, moreover, there were still the unruly American people. "Persuading the public" to abandon its prejudice against censorship would be impractical in light of the moral decline of the culture in recent decades. In providing a Bill of Rights that included the First Amendment, Eastland reminded us, the Founders counted on "a certain degree of virtue in the people," a condition that in his view can no longer be met. He refers to this state of affairs as "the disabling of America."

Then it is Irving Kristol's turn. The eminence grise of American neoconservatism could not have been happier with Lowenthal's authoritarian vision. "I want to welcome David Lowenthal to the Walter Berns-Robert Bork-Irving Kristol club," he wrote. "Each of us has, in the last three decades, argued in favor of censorship." (A recent conversation I had with Judge Bork, however, suggests that he has been having second thoughts about his membership in this club, precisely because of the use that is being made of its arguments by Clinton "liberals.") Like Bennett and Eastland, Kristol found the otherwise worthy project of censorship unworkable owing to the sorry state of the American people who cannot be counted on to support it.

Bizarrely, Kristol attributes this resistance to the influence of the post-1960s culture and the left's dominance of institutions like the American Bar Association, the law schools, and the media. These institutions, Kristol concluded, would crucify any nominee to the nation's higher courts who indicated a pro-censorship bias. Kristol is certainly right about liberal resistance to censorship when liberals are convinced the censor's axe will fall on the artistic avant-garde and other left-wing communities they favor. On the other hand, the left has already shown that it wants to censor the offensive speech it perceives in the mouths of its opponents as well as the violent imagery of the media in general.

Kristol failed to take into account that leftists can disagree among themselves and employ double standards that allow them to support the censorship of others while abhorring censorship of themselves. He seemed unaware of how his position makes him a bedfellow of feminist harridans like Andrea Dworkin and Catharine MacKinnon, and of moral busybodies like Hillary Clinton and Tipper Gore.

Among the commentators assembled by the *Standard*, only Cornell professor Jeremy Rabkin seemed to appreciate that the censors who would implement Lowenthal's proposal would inevitably be drawn from the class of political missionaries and commissars whose passion in life is to tell the rest of us how to live. "The people prepared to take the job would be ideologues—mostly of the crazy left, perhaps also of the religious right, but certainly ideologues," he wrote. Censorship by such zealots, Rabkin recognized, is "a recipe for a very nasty sort of politics and is sure to be self-defeating." Again, the strongest criticism that can be mustered against this protofascist agenda is its impracticality.

What is going on here? What happened to the conservative attitude that government cannot tie its shoelaces without putting entire populations in danger? How is it that a government unable to hand out money to poor people without destroying families and communities in the process can be entrusted with the infinitely more complex task of deciding what is morally healthy for 270 million diverse people to hear and see? How could any selfrespecting conservative not be repelled by a social prescription like Lowenthal's that overlooks these little problems of social engineering?

For that matter, how could any conservative not be appalled by his analysis of the problem itself? Since when, for example, have the media become "the primary educational force in the country," as he asserts? In educating the young, the primary educational force is and always has been the family. That is almost the primary principle of conservatism itself. It is also the only explanation for the fact that that the same "violent" television shows and movies are seen in America's violent inner cities and placid middle-class suburbs. Despite the claims of academic pseudoscience, normal individuals are not "desensitized" by fantasy acts of violence and transformed into homicidal maniacs. It is only sociopaths who confuse fantasy violence with reality. Are we now going to define the parameters of American freedom by the standard of the sociopaths among us? Now *that* is a truly liberal idea.

When all is said and done, the very image of Hollywood that governs the analyses of the would-be censors is itself a fantasy. Lowenthal asks: "Is fanning the flames of selfish and irresponsible lust, as obscenity does, not dangerous to our society? How can we expect the sexes to treat each other with decency and respect, the very young to forbear from sexual intercourse, and the family to remain stable in mutual devotion if sex detached from any sense of responsibility and even from love is touted daily in theaters and on television screens?" This is not only a false analysis of what we see and hear in theaters and on our television screens, it is ludicrous. Most prime-time television hours produced by the seven networks are saturated with sitcoms, whose invariable themes are celebrations of love, family, friendship, tolerance, loyalty, respect, and other timeless conservative virtues. More than a dozen networks—Family, Public Broadcasting, Disney, Discovery, History, Learning, c-span, pax—are even exclusively devoted to family-friendly and educational programming. Outside the news shows, rare incidents on late-night law and order series, and the occasional rerun of a feature film, there is virtually no violence to speak of on network television. As for feature films shown in theaters—do we really need to remind ourselves of this obvious fact?—these are seen only as the result of individual choices. A ticket purchase is required for entry. Do Americans really need censors to tell them what to choose?

There is a deeper and more troubling flaw in the social model inspiring these modern Savanarolas. If the tobacco, gun, and film industries are giant enterprises in a free-market system, it means that vast numbers of people want the products they offer. In a democracy, the people are sovereign. That is the American contract. If enough people find cigarettes, guns, and bad Hollywood pictures morally repulsive, such products will cease to be produced. That is the old-fashioned, but tested, remedy. Conservatives, more than anyone else, should know (and believe) this. Elites of all political persuasions may find democracy offensive to their own sensibilities and ideas. Sometimes, they may even make common cause with their ideological enemies to force their ideas of what is best on everybody else. But, for the sake of our democracy and ourselves, it would be unwise for the rest of us to humor them.

III

Hating Whitey

3

Guns Don't Kill Blacks,
Other Black People Do

T HE NAACP, the National Association for the Advancement
of Colored People, describes itself as an organization of "half
a million adult and youth members [who] are the premier
advocates for social justice and equal opportunity." In June 1999, the
NAACP launched a new civil rights crusade. Its president, Kweisi
Mfume, announced the organization's plans to file an injunctive class
action suit against gun manufacturers "to force them to distribute
their product responsibly."

In making the announcement, Mfume cited the disparate impact of gun violence on young black males. The NAACP issued a
press release backing up Mfume's claim with statistics showing that
African American males between the ages of fifteen and twenty-
four are almost five times more likely to be injured by firearms than
white males in the same age group. "Firearm homicide has been the
leading cause of death among young African American males for
nearly thirty years," the NAACP stated.

Am I alone in thinking this a pathetic, absurd, and almost hilari-
ous demonstration of political desperation by the civil rights estab-

lishment? What's next? Will Irish Americans sue whiskey distillers? Will Jews sue the gas company?

In truth, black civil rights leaders have blazed a trail for the Irish, accusing white and Korean liquor vendors of "invading" black communities and intoxicating their inhabitants. Boycotts have followed these charges, and antiwhite, anti-Korean race riots as well. But who forces alcohol down reluctant throats? And who is firing the guns that make young black males almost five times more likely to be victims of violence than whites? The answer is other young blacks. Why, then, does the NAACP even make the comparison between gun deaths of blacks and whites, if not as a racist insinuation that whites are somehow the *cause* of those "disproportionate" violent deaths, just as whites are often the implied *cause* of every other social pathology that afflicts the African American community? In the sociology of the left, there cannot be a wound the black community inflicts on itself that is not ultimately the responsibility of malicious whites. To think otherwise would be to "blame the victim." Only mean-spirited conservatives would even think of doing that.

The fact is that while blacks make up only 12 percent of the population, they account for more than 46 percent of total violent crime and over 90 percent of the murders of blacks.* It is black criminals, not whites or gun manufacturers, who are responsible for the disproportionate gun deaths of young black males. A gun—do I really have to spell this out?—is inanimate. It takes a human brain to pull the trigger. Firearms don't kill people. Sociopaths do. If young black males abuse firearms in an irresponsible and criminal fashion, why should the firearm industry be held accountable? Why not their parents? Why not themselves?

---

* J. M. Brown, P. Langan, and D. Levin, "Felony Sentences in State Courts, 1996" (Bureau of Justice Statistics, May 1999).

Unfortunately, as a nation, we have become so trapped in the melodrama of black victimization and white "oppression" that we have reached a point where we are in danger of losing all sense of reality. If blacks are oppressed in America, why isn't there a black exodus to countries where they are not? Why do all those black Haitians want to come here? To be oppressed? In the grips of what can only be described as a politically inspired group psychosis, we find it increasingly natural to collude with demagogic race hustlers in supporting a fantasy in which African Americans are no longer responsible for anything negative they do, even to themselves.

If blacks constitute just under half the prison population, for example, that fact cannot be allowed to suggest that some segments of the black community might have a problem when it comes to raising their children to be law abiding members of society. Such a statistic can only be explained by the racism of a criminal justice system that incarcerates too many blacks. This kind of nonsense is now proposed on a regular basis by "civil rights" leaders across the political spectrum, from the racist bloviator Al Sharpton to the urbane and usually sensible president of the Urban League, Hugh Price. In the intimidating atmosphere that this consensus creates, to suggest the obvious—that too many blacks are in prison because too many blacks commit crimes—is to risk being identified as an apologist for racism and perhaps a closet racist oneself.

The NAACP's antigun lawsuit came on the heels of the crusade to defend crack dealers, because 90 percent of them are African American and their sentences are allegedly "too harsh." This insipid campaign was launched by Jesse Jackson at the Washington march organized by race-hater Louis Farrakhan. That 90 percent of crack cocaine dealers are black cannot be seen, of course, as a moral stain on those crack dealers or as a massive social problem for the communities that produce them. It can only be the result of a white legal system that stigmatizes crack as a more dangerous drug than the powder cocaine the white community favors for itself. Forget that the heavier penalties were originally demanded by black leaders who claimed that crack was associated with street violence in the black community and that the white criminal justice system did not care enough about its destructive consequences to make the penalties sufficiently harsh. That was then; this is now. And now, lessening the sentences that were previously raised has become a crusade for "social justice" that overshadows the need to combat crime. Because racial oppression is the main enemy, the villainy of the crack trade is transformed into yet another symbol of white malevolence.

This kind of race baiting pervades the political discourse. In a Christopher Hitchens column that appeared in the Internet magazine *Salon* on August 10, 1999, George W. Bush was labeled "Governor Death" because of his determination to carry out the law for capital crimes in the state of Texas. The clear implication of Hitchens's attack was that Bush was collusive in a racist justice system in Texas that executes blacks in disproportionate numbers. "Perhaps you wonder if capital punishment is unevenly applied, as respects race and class, in the state of Texas," wrote Hitchens. "Wonder no longer. Just read the Amnesty report *Killing With Prejudice: Race and the Death Penalty in the USA*."

I read the Amnesty report; maybe Hitchens should too. The report *does not even mention racial or class statistics in Texas* and could not possibly be used to draw Hitchens's conclusion. Moreover, a perusal of the report reveals no self-evident truths even nationally. Like many "reports" about race these days, its treatment of the evidence is sloppy and its claims inflammatory.

Under the heading "Racist Representation of Indigent Defendants," for example, the Amnesty report offers the following evidence: "Gary Burns, black, executed in Indiana on 20 November 1997, was described to the jury by his white attorney as an 'insignificant, snivelly little street person.'" What is this supposed to prove? Maybe the attorney was trying to suggest that someone else must have done the deed of which his client was too weak to be guilty. Who can tell from this example? Most of the report consists of unsystematic and frustratingly brief snippets of cases just like this, along with a sprinkling of unanalyzed statistics that are presented in behalf of a partisan agenda.

It is true that the number of blacks executed in Texas (and nationwide) is greater than their proportion in the population. But it is also true that the number of black murderers far exceeds the proportion of blacks in the population at large. According to a Bureau of Justice Statistics Report on 1996 Trends (released May 1999), blacks commited 54 percent of the homicides in America even though they constituted only 12 percent of the population. An individual black male was eight times more likely to commit murder than an individual white male. Thus, in the most equitable system imaginable, a black male would be more likely than a white male to be executed.

In fact, however, convicted white murderers are more likely to be executed for their crimes than convicted black murderers. In 1996-1997, whites accounted for 62 percent of the convicted murderers executed in Texas. According to statistics provided by the Justice Department, the proportion of whites presently on death row compared to the total white population is almost four times that of the comparable proportion of blacks on death row in terms of the total black population. Whatever these statistics prove, they do not prove that justice in America is systemically biased against blacks.

Actually, the Amnesty report does not explicitly claim that there is a racial bias against African American *defendants* in murder cases (although it implies just that). The reason is that most studies of racial sentencing, including the "Baldus study," which is the one most frequently invoked by antideath-penalty activists, have found "neither strong nor consistent" evidence of discrimination directed against black defendants because of race.* But the desperation to prove white guilt is so great that instead of celebrating this as a triumph of civil rights reform, the race baiters merely shift their focus to the *victims* of capital crimes.

The statistic with which Amnesty opens its argument is this: "Of the five hundred prisoners executed between 1977 and 1998, 81.8 percent were convicted of murdering a white person, even though blacks and whites are the victims of homicide in almost equal numbers nationwide." No attempt is made, of course, to explain *how* the criminal justice system might systematically discriminate in favor of white victims but not *against* black defendants (except by this indirect method). What the report's raw statistics fail to take into account is that the death penalty is only imposed in aggravated circumstances, which can include the violence of the crime, whether it is committed in the course of another crime, or whether the perpetrator has a record of violent crimes. All these factors are ignored in the Amnesty report.

It so happens that black felons commit 43 percent of aggravated assaults, 66 percent of (armed) robberies, 27 percent of rapes and 85 percent of interracial crimes of violence, mainly against whites (this last figure from a Justice Department report for 1993). Since juries generally do not demand the death penalty for crimes of passion, where the victim is known to the killer, and since blacks are far more likely to commit violent crimes against whites than whites commit against blacks, the disparity that offends the Amnesty report has a basis in facts that may not imply a racial bias on the part of prosecutors and juries. The report does not acknowledge this problem.

---

* National Criminalization Victims Survey Report, 1993.

The defense of criminals as a civil rights cause is only an extreme manifestation of what has apparently become the very essence of the civil rights movement: blame whitey for problems endemic to the black community itself. Do black children fail to achieve in school? White oppression explains their failure. Poor black academic performance cannot be seen as a failure of black families to educate their children, or of the black community to support educational values, which are often referred to derisively as "thinking white." Black failure can only be the result of some lingering residue of the white perfidy involved in slavery and segregation. Call it "institutional racism."

Of course, those who invoke the phantom of "institutional racism" are too sophisticated to claim that there are actual racists lodged in our liberal education establishment who refuse to admit black children to legally integrated schools, or refuse to teach them when they get there. Instead, the concept of "institutional racism" is made to encompass an entire *system* of oppression that anonymously keeps black children down. It may do so through culturally rigged tests; or through the failure to provide black role models in positions of authority; or by providing underfunded schools to black neighborhoods; or as a result of the pervasive negative pressure exerted by an environment of poverty which cannot be countered with a mere six hours of school. (Compulsory preschool is already being proposed by the left as a new "right" and social cure-all, when the problem may not be school at all but lack of support in the community and the home.)

In reality, the failure of African American children to make the educational grade cannot be explained by *any* of these factors. Statistics anyalzed by the *New York Times* on July 4, 1999, dispel the poverty argument by establishing that impoverished white children whose parents earn less than ten thousand dollars a year score higher on standardized tests than black children whose parents earn more than seventy thousand dollars a year. None of these arguments, moreover, can explain why Vietnamese children who are poor and discriminated against, whose schools are underfunded and who are culturally at a greater disadvantage than blacks, and have fewer "role models," still manage to be educationally competitive.

While the oppression theme dominates public discourse, of course, no attention can be paid to the real problems that hold African American children back. There is a symbiosis, in fact, between the political mumbo jumbo of the Kweisi Mfumes and Jesse Jacksons (powerfully abetted by patronizing white liberals) and the seemingly intractable social problems in certain sectors of the black community. The myth of racial oppression, invoked to explain every social deficit of blacks, is an exercise in psychological denial. Crying racism deflects attention from the actual causes of the problems that afflict some African American communities. Its net result is to deprive people and communities who could help themselves of the power to change their fate.

Here are the facts: Nearly 70 percent of black children are born out of wedlock. A child raised in a single-parent, female-headed household is six times more likely to be poor than a child of any color born into a two-parent household. Seventy percent of youth violence is committed by males from female-headed households, regardless of race. If the NAACP and other black leaders want to end the terrible scourge of gun violence committed by young inner city blacks they should launch a campaign to promote marriage and family formation in the African American community; they should issue a moral plea to the community to stigmatize fathers who abandon their children and parents who have more children than they can afford. Instead of waging war against law enforcement agencies and supporting destructive racial demagogues like Al Sharpton, they should support the Rudy Giulianis and other advocates of public safety, whom they now attack. They should campaign for a tripling of police forces in inner city areas to protect the vast majority of inhabitants who are law-abiding and who are the true victims of the predators among them.

But to take these remedial steps would require rejecting the bogus charge of white oppression. It would mean abandoning the ludicrous claim that white America and firearms manufacturers are the cause of the problems afflicting African Americans. It would mean taking responsibility for their own communities instead.

It is true, of course, that when Jesse Jackson and other black leaders address their own communities they do recognize the real problems, the irresponsibility of absent fathers, the anti-educational attitudes in inner-city culture, the "black on black crime" that plagues inner-city neighborhoods. The problem is that messages conveyed by these admirable sermons are negated by the much louder irresponsible attacks on whites. You cannot focus attention on the problem of criminal predators in the African American community if you constantly proclaim the fundamental racism of the system that locks them up. You cannot combat the attitudes that undermine educational achievement among black children while you tell them that the tests were designed by racists to ensure that they will fail.

Given the enormous evident goodwill of white America towards blacks, the nation's commitment to combat discrimination in all its forms, the undeniable emergence of a successful black middle class, and the striking achievement of black political and cultural figures, why does the civil rights establishment perpetuate this myth of white oppression? Because the same establishment reaps great moral, psychological, and material rewards for doing so.

Blaming others for the failures and offenses that are one's own responsibility is a common human behavior. When it is reinforced, as it is in this case, by a patronizing liberal establishment, its payoffs can be irresistible. Racial ambulance chasing has allowed Jesse Jackson to live the life of a multimillionaire and catapulted Kweisi Mfume and others like him into the social and political stratosphere. Unfortunately, their successes have been at the expense of the truly disadvantaged African Americans their demagoguery leaves behind.

To take one example, the misdirected energies that have gone into creating, enforcing, and defending a system of racial preferences at American universities has had virtually no impact on the disadvantaged. *The Shape of the River*, by William Bowen and Derek Bok, studied the effect of race preferences at twenty-eight elite colleges. According to Bowen and Bok, 86 percent of the African American beneficiaries of these preferences came from households that were already middle class or affluent, while 64 percent had at least one parent who had been to college (a figure *six times* greater than the proportion for all college-age black youths).

In other words, without the race card so adeptly played by organizations like the NAACP, the already privileged families of the black middle class would have had to forego the additional government-provided privileges that the specter of white oppression justifies. Among these are free tuition, rigged entrance requirements, artificially inflated salaries, set-aside front companies and a variety of extortions too numerous to mention. These range from the outrageous sums provided to collegiate black student associations (to engage, among other things, the services of such racial hatemongers as Sister Souljah and Khalid Muhammad) to the ransoms paid by Texaco and other companies to forestall potentially damaging racial boycotts and often groundless discrimination suits. The continued suffering of disadvantaged black communities and the continued under-par performance of black school children is a price the well-heeled civil rights establishment is apparently willing to pay for guilt tributes from all-too-accommodating white "oppressors."

4

Racial Dialogue

THE PRECEDING CHAPTER originally appeared as a column in the Internet magazine *Salon* on August 16, 1999. Shortly afterwards, I received a phone call from a black columnist at *Time* magazine named Jack White, who wanted to interview me. I readily consented. The interview was not particularly unfriendly, but then journalists, as Janet Malcolm has reminded us, are often unprincipled seducers. In retrospect, I should be grateful for the hard edge to the voice on the other end of the line. It was the only honest treatment I was to receive from White.

In the course of our conversation, I disclosed to Jack White that I had been active in civil rights battles for more than fifty years, and that my extended family included members who were black. I also mentioned that I had recently conducted a crusade to keep a black talk show host on the air and that I was one of the most prominent advocates in the Republican Party of outreach to the black community. I also defended the bluntness of my attack on the current civil rights leadership by saying that I consider candor a sign of respect for people. It is the only way to talk about "racial issues" and get to the real problems at hand. Liberals, in my view, patronize blacks by talking down to them and by not telling them what they really think. The reason that many whites do not speak candidly, I told White, as I felt I had, is that they fear of being attacked as racists.

"Why do you think you can talk to black people like that?" White asked me when I was finished. "Because I paid my dues in the 1960s," I replied. "I have put myself on the line by devoting a good part of my political energies to fighting for the civil rights of African Americans. I think that earns me the right to speak frankly on these issues." When Jack White's column appeared in *Time* on August 30, 1999, our little exchange appeared at the conclusion of his piece in this sentence: "Last week Horowitz told me he had earned the right to talk down to blacks 'because of all I did in the '60s.'"

White's column was headlined "A Real, Live Bigot," and accused me, among other things, of suggesting that blacks leave the country if they do not like it: "If blacks are really oppressed in America, [Horowitz] asks, 'why isn't there a black exodus?' Well, what does Horowitz want us to do, go back to Africa?" This malicious distortion of what I had said reappeared in a letter to the editor by NAACP chairman Julian Bond, who referred to my statement as "Horowitz's invitation to black Americas to love America or leave it," and who accused me of being a "'60s turncoat" and a closet racist who had been outed.

It is not a pleasant experience to open *Time* magazine and see a picture of yourself under the heading "A Real, Live Bigot." It has the aura of an excommunication from the community of decency. The fear of such a fate undoubtedly works to prevent others from expressing their true feelings about issues that touch on the subject of race. *Time*'s audience of four million readers had no idea of who I was except for what Jack White had written. Fortunately, despite its massive circulation, *Time* no longer has the authority in American culture it once had. The explosion of new media channels and of the Internet in particular have ended the hold that institutions like *Time* and network television once had on the nation's attention.

After reading White's column, I called my friend Matt Drudge, whose website is widely consulted by members of the media and receives a million hits daily (making it almost comparable in readership to *Time*). I told him I was contemplating a libel suit against the magazine and Jack White. I also e-mailed him a lengthy response to White's charges in an open letter to *Time*'s managing editor, Walter Isaacson, along with a demand for a retraction. Drudge immediately posted my response. I then posted these materials on my own website, at frontpagemag.com, along with an appeal to readers to e-mail Isaacson to protest White's attack.

A black journalists' association sent an e-mail to its members claiming that the libel suit I was contemplating against White was "an attack on the First Amendment rights of all African American journalists." This made no sense unless all African American journalists had the same disregard for truth as Jack White, and not even then. What it did reveal was the paranoid racial sensibility of the leaders of this association.

In fact, I had no serious intention of filing a suit. As I already knew, the libel laws, as presently construed, would view this slander as "opinion" and therefore nonactionable. But it was a device to gain attention for my defense. Howard Kurtz, the media critic of the *Washington Post*, was one of a number of reporters who picked up the story, accomplishing my main objective which was to get my response—or pieces of it—before as large an audience as possible. A great boost to this effort came when my liberal editors at *Salon* sprang to my defense, printing my response for their one-and-a-half million readers and making strong declarations in my behalf. It was a novel experience, accustomed as I am to being mercilessly attacked from the left. More than two thousand *Salon* readers, many of whom undoubtedly disagree with me on many issues, sent e-mails of protest to *Time*.

Perhaps the most gratifying response came from one of the most extraordinary intellectual voices of our time, Camille Paglia, my fellow columnist at *Salon*:

> I respect the astute and rigorously unsentimental David Horowitz as one of America's most original and courageous political analysts. He has the true 1960s spirit—audacious and irreverent, yet passionately engaged and committed to social change.
>
> Although we are both columnists for *Salon*, I do not know Horowitz—aside from when I was interviewed on his radio show in California eight years ago. But I regard him as an important contemporary thinker who is determined to shatter partisan stereotypes and to defy censorship wherever it occurs— notably, in this case, in the area of discourse on race, which is befogged with sanctimony and hypocrisy.
>
> As a scholar who regularly surveys archival material, I think that, a century from now, cultural historians will find David Horowitz's spiritual and political odyssey paradigmatic for our time.

It was worth getting slandered by Jack White to elicit a testimonial like that.

The efforts of my defenders got the attention of Isaacson, who sent columnist Margaret Carlson as an intermediary to an event I was holding in Colorado over Labor Day weekend. Our meeting led to a phone call from Isaacson and a meeting with *Time*'s editorial board in New York.

Isaacson is a reader of *Heterodoxy*, a magazine Peter Collier and I edit, and is familiar with my work. He had been out of town when White's column ran, acknowledged its unfairness, and was apologetic about any damage it might have done. "I was not as left as you in the Sixties," he said, "and I'm not as conservative as you now." Still, he did not want to make a formal apology for something a columnist had written. He felt it was an editor's responsibility to stand behind his columnists whatever their opinions and protect their journalistic freedom. He agreed to come to Los Angeles to speak at a luncheon forum I host called the Wednesday Morning Club and to assign a review of *Hating Whitey*, although he could not promise it would be favorable.

I respect Isaacson and, though I was not happy with his unwillingness to print a formal retraction, understood his reasoning. Nevertheless, I thought there was another factor at work, and I told him so. If he were to make such a retraction, there would be a political firestorm directed at him by the racial left and African American journalists in particular. *Time*, then, would have been the target of accusations similar to Jack White's against me. This, I said, was the essence of the problem everyone faces in addressing issues of race.

Time's review of *Hating Whitey*, written by Lance Morrow and entitled "Indignant Sanity," appeared on November 22, 1999. After referring to my "Whittaker Chambers-like conversion," Morrow wrote: "Horowitz is as much despised among [racial leftists] as Chambers was at Georgetown dinner parties during the Alger Hiss case years ago. Among racial intellectuals, Horowitz is 'Not Our Class, Dear.' *Hating Whitey*—with its inflammatory title—deserves a reading. Horowitz is angry and polemical, but he is also a clear and ruthless thinker. What he says has an indignant sanity about it. For cautionary perspective in an argument like this, it pays to remember that Hiss was guilty and Chambers was right."

With the appearance of Morrow's review, I felt that my reputation was restored. This feeling was strengthened by the many appearances I made on radio and television where I was able to present my case to millions of Americans. One such appearance was an hour-long talk show on Black Entertainment Television hosted by Tavis Smiley. The entire program was devoted to a discussion of the themes of *Hating Whitey*—the betrayal of the civil rights movement by demagogic leaders like Al Sharpton and Jesse Jackson, the fact that black leaders blame white people for problems endemic to the black community, and the acceptance of antiwhite racism by the liberal culture.

As a condition of my appearance on the show, I had asked that Larry Elder, a black libertarian talk show host, be invited as well. Smiley readily consented and proved to be a gracious and professional host. One of the questions I was glad to have Larry field was: "Don't you think racism is the number one problem for African Americans?" "No I don't," he responded. "Crime, drugs, education, and the dissolution of the family are far more important problems for the African American community than white racism."

Our opponent was a postmodernist professor named Michael Eric Dyson, who confronted us with one left-wing cliché about race after another, but formulated them in an academic *patois* that no normal human being could understand. A phone survey, conducted throughout the hour among the show's live television audience, asked the following question: "Do black people blame whites too much for their problems?" At the end of the show, the poll results were put up on the screen revealing that 62 percent of the mostly black audience had voted "Yes," while only 38 percent said "No."

. . . . .

One of the irate letters *Salon* received in response to my original column was from an angry Chicago reader named Alice Huber, who introduced herself as an African American woman married to a white man. According to her, I was indeed a "bigot" and, moreover, a bigot of "the worst kind." In her eyes, I had earned the label "racist" that Jack White had pinned on me by suggesting that blacks might no longer be "oppressed" in America and by questioning whether white racism was the immediate or principal cause of problems afflicting black youth like violence and educational failure. Adding insult to injury was my claim to solidarity in the struggle for equal rights. "Horowitz says he earned the right to talk to blacks 'honestly,'" Huber wrote, "because of the '60s. Personally, I don't care how many marches he went to, how much money he dropped in a civil rights bucket, how many times he sang 'We Shall Overcome' with guest celebrities; Horowitz is not black, and he has no right to tell me or any other person of color how to pursue issues pertaining to our communities."

This attitude is not original with Alice Huber (which is the reason I insisted on having Larry Elder as an ally on the Tavis Smiley show). It is an argument familiar to anyone who has engaged black Americans in recent decades over issues of race : "If you don't walk in my shoes, you can't feel my pain." The conclusion that is supposed to follow from this observation is usually presented as self-evident: "If you can't feel my pain, you can't tell me how I should deal with it."

This was indeed the text of many a political sermon when objections were raised to the "Million Man March" because it was organized and led by Louis Farrakahn, an anti-Semitic racist. "Don't tell us what leaders to choose or what marches to join," was a response heard from many otherwise sensible black commentators. It's a "black thing." It's a matter of community pride: "We're not listening when white people tell us what to do anymore; we're not letting you choose our leaders." Indeed, marching behind such an unpalatable figure as Farrakhan was itself a way of emphasizing black independence and the degree to which African Americans had liberated themselves from white tutelage.

The same attitude was evident at the time of the O. J. Simpson verdict, when black leaders showed not the slightest embarrassment at the spectacle of African American communities all over the country cheering the acquittal of the accused, a demonstration of striking insensitivity and bad taste. Imagine the reaction of black leaders if there had been a similar response to the release of a white defendant accused of murdering his black wife and a black stranger, particularly if the white defendant had no credible alibi, was confronted by overwhelming DNA evidence, and had a record of beating his black spouse prior to her death. A triumphal response to such an acquittal would have been taken as self-evidently racist. But in the Simpson affair, the response of the African American community was: "We don't care what you think or what you feel. What we feel is all that matters. No one—least of all any white—is going to tell us how to behave." Imagine if the colors had been reversed.

This cold-hearted calculus is a central theme of what is now generously described as "black separatism," but is more accurately seen as a species of racism. As an attitude it is deep and widespread in the African American community, and is growing as a sentiment as well. A recent poll by the NAACP reported that over 40 percent of blacks and 50 percent of whites now accept the doctrine of racially separate but equal. There should be no surprise in this, given the official sanction of self-segregation for blacks in universities, once the most liberal institutions of our culture.

Whites have their own segregationist impulses, but the license that the black leadership has given to the idea of separatism among the educated classes—white and black—can hardly have been without impact. Perhaps out of guilt, or perhaps because they do not care, whites have been willing to go along with what the African

American community wants in these matters, without regard to their own standards of what is appropriate, moral, or good. If blacks want to march behind a racist like Farrakhan, fine. If they want racially segregated graduations and racially segregated dormitories and racially oriented curricula in the schools, okay. If they want to bring back the segregationist standard of "separate but equal," that must be all right too.

As we divide along racial lines and increasingly surrender the ability to speak with a communal voice, we are losing the fundamental idea of what it means to be American. This is the idea that all men—regardless of race, color, or creed—are created equal, and must be equal before the law. The Founders did not say "all white men are equal"; the words "black" and "white" do not appear in the Constitution. They did not say "all Americans are created equal" or all Christians or all Europeans. They said "all" without exception.

The implications of separatism are fundamentally subversive of the American idea, but also of the moral ideal that has been responsible for the liberation of black people from their oppressions, first as slaves, and then as second-class citizens. If the white majority had been unable to feel blacks' pain, they would not have responded as they did to the injustices they or their ancestors inflicted and which brought many of them material advantages and privilege.

It is, of course, not just whites who cannot actually *feel* blacks' pain. The fact is that nobody can *feel* anybody's pain but one's own. This paradox is a timeless theme of Western epistemology going back at least to Descartes, who believed that the only reality that is certain is the interior knowledge we have of our own feelings and thoughts. But, taken to its logical extreme, this solipsistic viewpoint and the relativist perspective it inspires would mean the end of any ethical outlook. It would preclude the possibility of any appeal to morality or conscience, and thus the possibility of society itself.

How can any morality exist if you have to actually be in another's shoes to feel his pain? How can we know that slavery is wrong, if we have not been slaves? That discrimination is wrong if we have not been discriminated against? How can we feel compelled to do unto others as we would have them do unto us, if there is no commonality between us? Yet the very idea of that kinship in our common humanity is what motivated Wilberforce and other white Christians to end the slave trade. How could they (or we) know or feel that an injustice has been done to others if those others are so alien that we cannot identify with them?

Take this a step further: How can blacks presume to tell whites what is right or wrong for them—which is what the entire civil rights discourse has been about—if being different disqualifies anyone from making such statements? How can blacks appeal to the conscience of whites in seeking to be treated as equals, if they reject the very concept of common humanity that underpins the principle of equality? In short, how can blacks expect justice from us, if we cannot expect it from them? If we cannot imagine what it is like to be them, what are they appealing to when they ask for justice and respect? "There, but for the grace of God go I" is mankind's fundamental ethical intuition. If we cannot imagine ourselves in the place of another, what sympathy can we have for him? What kinship can we feel? How can we regard them as brothers and sisters under the skin?

We cannot. And that is the problem for those who employ the separatist argument. Admittedly, as in all such arguments, there is a kernel of truth in the separatist complaint. Life experiences are different, and such differences are important. They form the basis of much of the intellectual disagreement over race and provide the ground of our pluralistic identity as Americans. But the basis of our

American identity is also an injunction to accept these differences in order to reach each other across the boundaries they create: *e pluribus unum*. Out of many cultures and many ethnicities, one.

It is crucial to the moral community we strive to maintain that our differences have limits and that they be checked against sympathies that are manifest. If I show care for you, I probably have a capacity to empathize with your experience and understand who you are. It is your ability to recognize this and to listen to me (and my ability to listen to you) that forms the basis of our coexistence. But if you ignore me and my concerns, you invite a similar response from me. In fact, if you show hostility to me, I am probably not going to care as much about you as I otherwise might. Moreover, I may be tempted to reciprocate. The hostility of black separatists to non-blacks is certainly a cause of the lack of sympathy that separatist blacks experience. What you give is often what you get. In recent decades, there has been a palpable decline in the sympathy that non-African Americans feel for the agendas of the civil rights movement. This is directly related to the growth of separatist feelings and antiwhite rhetoric in the African American community and to the perversion of the civil rights agenda into separatist grievances.

The civil rights movement Martin Luther King led was based on the old single-standard ethics and the old goal of integration. It was supported by large majorities in the Congress and by the overwhelming majority of the white population. The same cannot be said for the civil rights policies of the current African American leadership. There will not be broad support for the NAACP's suits against gun manufacturers or educational test providers. The racial preferences that are currently considered the *sine qua non* of a civil rights loyalty are rejected by almost as large majorities among non-African Americans as once supported the civil rights agenda of Martin Luther

King. Recognizing this, African Americans have to ask themselves whether this is the result of racist attitudes on the part of whites or whether it is a failure of their own leadership to articulate worthy agendas.

If Alice Huber and Jack White want to call someone as committed to civil rights issues as myself a "racist" because I disagree with their assessment of some racial grievances, they must bear responsibility for the decreasing power of the term itself. The reality is that the accusation of racism has lost a great deal of its sting in recent decades through its abusive use by demagogues. If Jack White, a prime offender in these matters, had written his slander for the *Village Voice* or the *Amsterdam News*, no one would have paid any attention. Those institutions have so abused the term by applying it frivolously to political opponents that only their own constituencies find their usage credible anymore. It is only the authority of *Time* that gave White's slanders any weight. If *Time* were to continue to publish racial rants like White's, on the other hand, its own credibility would rapidly diminish.

Drawing their inspiration from the ideas of Malcolm X, the current African American leadership has squandered the moral capital that Martin Luther King accumulated, undermining the civil rights cause they claim to support. Ask yourself which current African American civil rights leader has significant respect among communities that are not black or politically to the left. Certainly not Kweisi Mfume, Julian Bond, or Jesse Jackson, whose moral authority among most Americans is virtually nonexistent. Under their leadership the African American community has steadily isolated itself and diminished its political base, while reviving its own segregation.

These are lessons to ponder, and not only for Alice Huber and Jack White.

. . . . .

Within weeks of Jack White's attack, I published a book called *Hating Whitey and Other Progressive Causes*. Even before publication, the book had encountered the same difficulties as my article.

The New York publishing house that had released my previous books refused to publish this one. Although I had made my former publisher over half a million dollars in revenues on *Radical Son* and *The Politics of Bad Faith*, my editor told me that they "will never publish a book with that title." When it finally appeared under another imprint, the student paper at the University of Michigan refused to run a paid advertisement for the book, even though the same paper had run advertisements by anti-Semitic Holocaust-deniers and defended the decision to do so as "freedom of the press." Several bookstore managers also said they would refuse to stock the book because of the title.

Why is *Hating Whitey* such a controversial title? Are there no haters of white people? Doesn't the Nation of Islam preach that all whites are "devils" and will be destroyed by God in a coming Armageddon? Didn't the late jazz great Miles Davis tell an interviewer (to cite but one example among many) that he would rather be alone on a desert island than have the company of someone who was white? Many otherwise intelligent people have attempted to dismiss the problem of black racism by claiming that only white people can be racists since "blacks don't have power." As though there were no black elected officials in America, or black corporate executives, or black military officers, or black law enforcement officials with power over whites.

In refusing my advertisement the *Michigan Daily*'s spokesman explained that my title "might offend some of our students," making it clear he meant white students. But why would white students who have suffered from antiwhite racism be offended by a book that objected to antiwhite racism? In fact, only leftist whites who consider themselves "progressive" would find the contents of *Hating Whitey* unpalatable.

The reason *Hating Whitey* is controversial is that it confronts the central hypocrisy of our political culture. As Americans, we insist that it is wrong to denigrate any ethnic group. But out of the other side of our collective mouth, we often speak as though white people are racists and "oppressors" and can be blamed for every problem that afflicts minorities, especially blacks. That is, for instance, the deplorable message of the NAACP's lawsuit against the educational testing services. How is blaming tests, going to help African American youngsters to pass them? It isn't.

Hating Whitey and Other Progressive Causes is unacceptable to liberals because it puts them up against a dilemma they themselves have created. Why wasn't there a collective guffaw when the NAACP announced suits against gun manufacturers and testing services? Why did no one say: It is time to retire the present civil rights leadership, which has become a ridiculous and divisive social force? Why did no one protest the hurtful messages the NAACP is sending to minority youth who are afflicted by violence and unable to compete educationally?

The reason for the silence is the stigma incurred by those who do actually object. That is why I insisted on calling my book *Hating Whitey* even though I knew it meant losing my publisher. The fear we have of identifying the real problems is paralyzing our ability to confront them. Only when enough people refuse to be intimidated can this situation be changed. The title I chose was my way of forcing the issue.

. . . . .

Shortly after the publication of *Hating Whitey*, Jesse Jackson interposed himself into a high school disciplinary case in Decatur, Illinois. In the wake of his intervention, people could be forgiven for suspecting that I had hired him to promote my book.

Jackson went to Decatur to defend seven delinquents involved in a gang fight at a high school football game, which had spread panic through the stands, endangering the safety of innocent bystanders, including women and children. Apparently the incident was a rumble between members of the Gangster Disciples and the Vice Lords (interesting self-revelations of those involved). Nonetheless, Jackson consistently referred to the brawlers as "our children," presenting them as victims whom the white majority on the Decatur school board was persecuting by denying them access to educational opportunity.

The six white members of the Decatur school board had reacted swiftly to the incident. They had expelled the delinquents in an effort to punish them according to the school rules, while making them an example to others. Like many other school boards, Decatur's had adopted a policy of "zero tolerance for violence" in the wake of the Columbine shootings and similar terrifying incidents at high schools across America. Discipline, it should hardly need saying, is an absolutely crucial element in the creation of a learning environment. Youngsters who go to school in fear are not going to be able to focus on their studies. Youngsters who do not respect authority are not going to learn.

There is no sector of the population that needs to hear and heed these messages more than young inner-city African American males. One in three among them is a convicted felon. Homicide is their number one cause of death, and their killers are mainly other young African American males. It takes no genius to see that restoring social and individual discipline in the inner city (that is, having a zero tolerance for violence) is the most crucial task facing this community if it is to increase the life chances of its most disadvantaged members. Yet here was Jesse Jackson in Decatur, breaking the law in a protest to support criminal rioters, and attempting to turn them into civil rights heroes.

In Decatur, Jesse Jackson abused the civil rights movement, just as over the years he has squandered the moral legacy that the movement inherited from its founder, turning "civil rights" into a ritual of blame. "The march on Selma had to do with access to voting, equal protection under the law," Jackson intoned in one of his absurd statements to the press. "The march on Washington: access to public accommodation, equal protection under the law. In Decatur: access to quality education for all children, equal protection under the law."

This is just doublespeak, an American update of the Orwellian slogan "slavery is freedom." Quality education and equal protection under the law are precisely what the white members of the Decatur school board were defending for all their students, white and black. The charge that the legal authorities laid against Jackson when he was arrested in Decatur was perfectly apt: "contributing to the delinquency of a minor."

What has happened to the civil rights movement? For several decades it has been clear that "civil rights" leaders like Jesse Jackson have run out of legitimate causes. From Tawana Brawley to O. J. Simpson, from suits against gun manufacturers to support for racial preferences and racial census categories, the civil rights movement has become first a caricature and then an outright betrayal of its former self.

Under the new dispensation, Al Sharpton—anti-Semite, freelance racist, and convicted liar—is now part of the "civil rights leadership." He is accepted in this role as an African American spokesman by Democratic presidential candidates Bill Bradley and

Al Gore, and by First Lady Hillary Clinton. But Sharpton has merely trod the path that Jesse Jackson and other mainstream leaders had previously beaten smooth for him. It was Jackson and NAACP chief Kweisi Mfume, for example, who embraced the race-hater Farrakhan before Sharpton, and made it clear that no moral lines would be drawn within the black community but only as between blacks and whites. That is a racist idea in itself.

What a contrast between this moral myopia and the high standard set by Martin Luther King, who refused to appear on any public platform beside Malcolm X because of the racism Malcolm X preached. The purpose of that ostracism was to draw a clear moral line between what the civil rights movement stood for and what it was against. Under King's leadership, the civil rights movement was as opposed to black racists like Malcolm X as it was to bigots who were white. It was a matter of principle.

In those days, no civil rights leader made excuses for the bad behavior of individual blacks because they were black. No civil rights leader invoked "four hundred years of slavery" to exculpate criminals, or claimed that blacks themselves could not be racist, or that juvenile delinquents were merely victims of white disciplinarians. In those days, civil rights leaders laid down a single standard for all, regardless of race, color, or creed.

Their collective stand had real-world consequences. Malcolm X gave up his bigotry and paid King the homage he deserved. When Malcolm renounced his racism in his last year of life, King agreed to be seen and photographed alongside him. But this very picture has now become an icon of their relationship. The false memory has erased the distinction that King worked so diligently to make, as though their original conflict never took place. In the years since King's death, Malcolm X has been raised to canonic status as a patron saint of the civil rights movement. But it was a movement for which he had contempt and which he strenuously opposed, because he had no faith in the humanity of white America to respond to King's call and give justice to blacks. Malcolm X was wrong; King was right. It is time for African Americans to acknowledge this truth.

Instead, the blurring of distinctions between King and Malcolm X has become a template for the moral confusion that has overtaken the civil rights movement and led it astray. Perhaps the most depressing sign of this disorder is the absence of prominent voices from within the African American community dissenting from its tragic betrayal. Not since the death of Congresswoman Barbara Jordan has there been an African American leader with the courage to call the wayward movement to account in the terms necessary. In a memorable keynote at the Democratic convention of 1984 she declared: "We are one, we Americans; we are one. And we reject any intruder who seeks to divide us on the basis of race and color. We must not allow ideas like political correctness to divide us and cause us to reverse hard-won achievements in human rights and civil rights. We reject both white racism and black racism. Our strength in this country is rooted in our diversity—our history bears witness to that fact. *E pluribus unum*, from many, one. It was a good idea when the country was founded, and it's a good idea today." Here is the heroic voice of a black leadership that is currently missing among us, the only voice to which Americans who are not African American and who are not politically left will respond, the only voice capable of leading Americans towards an integrated future.*

---

*   There are, of course, courageous and authentic black American voices that have carried forward the Jordan standard—Ward Connerly, Clarence Thomas, J. C. Watts, Thomas Sowell, Walter Williams, Shelby Steele, to name a few. But they are cut off from significant constituencies in the African American community through the collusion of the black civil rights leadership and their white liberal allies in the media, the universities, and the Democratic Party.

There are plenty of racial incidents in America today that require vigilant public attention. But people of all colors and all ethnicities perpetrate these incidents. What this nation needs, as Barbara Jordan so eloquently declared, is a single standard for every American when judging what is just and unjust. If discipline works for white youngsters, it should work for black youngsters as well, Jesse Jackson and his allies notwithstanding. If it is wrong to hate "people of color" and to scapegoat them for every social problem, it is equally wrong to hate white people and scapegoat them. Jesse Jackson and other civil rights leaders would serve the cause of justice far better if they would return to the single standard proclaimed in the Constitution and realized in the civil rights struggles of the 1960s under the leadership of Dr. King.

IV

Radical Pursuits

5

The Intellectual Class War

A FEW YEARS AFTER THE FALL of the marxist utopias, I found myself in Beverly Hills sitting next to a man who was worth half a billion dollars. His name was Stanley Gold, and he was chairman of a holding company that was the largest shareholder in Disney, at the time the largest media corporation in the world. Since I was engaged in a conservative project in the entertainment community and the occasion was a cocktail reception for a Republican senator, I quickly turned the conversation into a pitch for support. But I was only able to run through a few bars of my routine before Gold put a fatherly hand on my arm and said, "Save your breath, David. I'm a socialist."

I am reminded of this story every time a leftist critic assaults me (which is often) and deploys the marxist cliché that I have "sold out" my ideals, or suggests that an opinion I have expressed can be explained by the "fact" that somewhere a wealthy puppetmaster is pulling my strings. I am not alone, of course, in being the target of such ad hominem slanders, which are familiar to every conservative who has ever engaged in a political debate.

Of course, those who traffic in socially-conscious abuse have a ready answer for anecdotes like mine, namely, that it is an aberration. Even if it is true, therefore, it is false because there is a larger marxist "truth" that trumps little facts like this. This truth is that conservative ideas express the views of corporate America, serve the status quo, defend the rich and powerful, and legitimize the oppression of the poor. Whereas leftist views, however well paid for, are noble because they oppose all the injustice that corporate America, the status quo, and the rich represent. The "truth" is that conservative views *must* be paid for because they could not possibly be the genuine views of any decent human being with a grain of integrity or compassion.

In the fantasy world of the left, the figure of Stanley Gold can only be understood as a human oxymoron: a good-hearted capitalist who is a friend to humanity and a traitor to his class. But, then, so are such famous left-wing moguls as Ted Turner, David Geffen, Oprah Winfrey, Steven Spielberg, Michael Eisner, and a hundred others less famous (but equally wealthy) that one could easily name.

In fact, Stanley Gold is exceptional only in his wit and candor— and his ideological frame of mind. For, unlike the self-identified progressives named above, the CEOs of most major corporations studiously avoid ideological politics, left or right, because such politics are not in the corporate interest. To become identified with a hard political position is to become a target for opponents who control the machinery of regulation and taxation and exert life-and-death power over business. Moreover, from a business point of view most politicians are fungible: the kind of favors businesses require can be performed by one politician as easily as another. It is safer to stay above the fray and buy politicians when necessary, Republicans as well as Democrats, conservatives and liberals. Money, not ideological passion, is the currency of corporate interest, power rather than ideas its political agenda. Therefore, politicians rather than intellectuals are the normal objects of its attention.

There are two exceptions to this rule of political neutrality. First, when an administration, for whatever reason, chooses to declare war on a wealthy individual, corporation, or even an entire industry, embracing the political opposition may seem the best option in an already bad situation. Big Tobacco, Microsoft, and Michael Milken, for example, when assaulted by government, adopted this defensive strategy (Tobacco and Microsoft went strongly Republican; Milken became a Democrat). Second, when political activists shake down a large corporation, a tactic almost exclusively of the left, the corporation will choose to underwrite their group. Under attack from radical Greens, for example, major companies like ARCO have become large subsidizers of the environmental movement. Through similar extortionist efforts, Jesse Jackson's Rainbow/Push coalition has received more corporate underwriting than any dozen conservative groups put together.

Nevertheless, the norm for corporate interests remains the removal of themselves and their assets from ideological politics. The same applies to individuals who are serious financial players. I have had very conservative billionaires tell me that whatever their personal views, they cannot afford to be political (in my sense) at all.

A consequence of this standoff is that most of the contributions available to ideological activists of the left or right are either small individual donations solicited through direct mail campaigns or large institutional donations from tax-exempt foundations. In this area, too, the fevered imaginations of the left have created a wildly distorted picture in which well-funded goliaths of the right, Olin, Scaife and Bradley, overwhelm the penurious Davids of the left. Edward Said, for example, used the platform of the once distinguished Reith lectures to attack Peter Collier and myself over the "second thoughts" movement we launched years ago as a critique of the left: "In a matter of months during the late 1980s, Second Thoughts aspired to become a movement, alarmingly well funded by right-wing Maecenases like the Bradley and Olin Foundations. . . ."

Some years later, a report appeared, "The Strategic Philanthropy of Conservative Foundations," documenting the annual disbursements of what were deemed to be the key conservative grant-giving institutions. The annual sum of the subsidies from twelve conservative foundations was seventy million dollars. This amount may seem large until one looks at the Ford Foundation, which dispenses all by itself more than five hundred million dollars each year—more than seven times as much—mainly to liberal and leftwing causes. Ford is the principal funder, for example, of the hard-left Mexican American Legal Defense Fund (MALDEF), which lacks any visible base in the Mexican American community, but has been the principal promoter of illegal immigration and the driving force behind the failed multibillion-dollar bilingual education programs. Ford created MALDEF and has provided it with more than twenty-five million dollars over the years. Ford has also been the leading funder of left-wing feminism and black separatism on American campuses, and of the radical effort to balkanize our national identity through multicultural university curricula.

Ford is typical. The biggest and most prestigious foundations, bearing the names of the most venerable captains of American capitalism—Ford, Rockefeller, Mellon, Carnegie, and Pew—are all biased to the left, as are many newer but also well-endowed institutions like the MacArthur, Markle, and Schumann foundations. MacArthur alone is three times the size of the "big three" conservative foundations—Olin, Bradley, and Scaife—combined.

Moreover, these foundations do not represent the most important support the corporate "ruling class" and its social elites provide to the left. That laurel goes to the private and public universities that have traditionally been the preserve of the American aristocracy and now, as Richard Rorty has happily pointed out, are the "political base of the left." With its multibillion-dollar endowment and unmatched intellectual prestige, Harvard provides an exemplary case, its relevant faculties and curricula reflecting the absolute hegemony of left-wing ideas. The Kennedy School of Government at Harvard is arguably the most prestigious and important reservoir of intellectual talent and policy counsel available to the political establishment. Cabinet officials are regularly drawn from its ranks. Of its more than 150 faculty members, only five are identifiable Republicans, a ratio that is extraordinary given the spectrum of political opinion in the nation at large. Yet it is the rule in the university system.

The institutional and financial support for the left—through its dominance in the universities, the book publishing industry, the press, television news, and the arts—is so overwhelming it is hardly contested. There are no prestigious universities where the faculty ratio in the liberal arts and social sciences is 150 Republicans to five Democrats. There is not a single major American newspaper whose features and news sections are written by conservatives rather than liberals—and this includes such conservative-owned institutions as the *Wall Street Journal*, the *Los Angeles Times*, whose editorial pages are left wing as well, the *Orange County Register*, and the *San Diego Union*.

Some will object to my definition of what is "left" as a way of avoiding the irrefutable reality it describes. They will argue that because Noam Chomsky is regarded as a fringe intellectual by segments of the media, the media cannot be dominated by the ideas of the left. But this supposes that Chomsky's exclusion is ideological rather than idiosyncratic. After all, Peter Jennings is a fan of Cornel West who is a fan of Noam Chomsky's. Christopher Hitchens is a fan of Noam Chomsky and ubiquitous on television and in print. Regardless, the fact remains that an America-loathing crank like Chomsky is an incomparably more influential intellectual figure in the left-wing culture of American universities than any conservative one could name.

The left, it can hardly be disputed, is funded and supported by the very "ruling class" it asserts is the puppetmaster of the right and the oppressor of minorities, the working class, and the poor. Institutional support and funds provided to the intellectual left by the "ruling class" far exceeds any sums it provides to the intellectual right, as any one with a pocket calculator will grasp. Why is this so? Could it be that the marxist model itself is nonsense?

It is hardly evident, for example, that the interest of the corporate rich lies in preserving the status quo. If the Clinton years did nothing else, they should certainly have served to put this canard to rest. The Clinton Administration's most important left wing projects were the comprehensive government-controlled healthcare plan, which failed, and the effort to preserve racial preferences, which succeeded. Both agendas received the enthusiastic support of corporate America—the health care plan from the nation's largest health insurance companies and racial preferences from Fortune 500 corporations across the board.

Or try another measure: in the 1999 presidential primary campaign, Bill Bradley was the Democratic candidate running from the left. The chief points of Bradley's platform were a revival of the comprehensive Clinton healthcare scheme and the pursuit of left wing racial grievances. Bradley's most recently acquired African American friend is the anti-Semitic racist Al Sharpton, the black leader of choice for Democratic Party candidates. But despite these radical agendas, as everyone knows, "Dollar Bill's" thirty-plus-million-dollar campaign war chest was largely filled by Wall Street, where he himself has made millions as a stockbroker over the years.

The explanation for the paradox is this: Unless one is seduced by the discredited poppycock of leftist intellectuals, there is no reason the rich should be adversaries of the poor or oppose their interests. Not in a dynamic market society like ours. Only if the market is a zero-sum game as marxists and their clones believe—"exploited labor" for the worker, "surplus value" for the capitalist—would leftist clichés make any sense. But they do not. The real-world relation between labor and capital is quite the opposite of what the left proposes. Entrepreneurs generally want a better-educated, better-paid, more diverse working force, because that means better employees, better marketers, and better consumers of the company product. That is why, historically, everywhere capitalism has been embraced, labor conditions have improved and inequalities have diminished whether there has been a strong trade union presence or not. That is why the capitalist helmsmen of the World Trade Organization are better friends of the world's poor than any of the Luddite demonstrators against them in Seattle.

The twenty-first century political argument is not about whether to help the poor, or whether to include all Americans in the social contract. Republicans embrace these objectives as firmly as Democrats, conservatives as well as liberals. The issue is how best to help the poor, how best to integrate the many cultures of the American mosaic into a common culture that works. Twenty years after the welfare system was already a proven disaster for America's inner city poor, Democrats and leftists were still demanding more welfare and opposing significant reforms. Clinton himself vetoed the Republicans reform bill twice and only signed it when he was told he would not be reelected if he did not. Welfare reform has liberated hundreds of thousands of poor people from dead-end dependency and given them a taste of the self-esteem that comes from earning one's keep.

If the left were serious about its interest in the poor, it would pay homage to the man who made welfare reform possible, the despised former Speaker Newt Gingrich. If hypocrisy were not their stock-in-trade, self-styled champions of the downtrodden like Cornel West and Marian Wright Edelman would be writing testimonials to Newt Gingrich as a hero to America's poor. But that will not happen. Instead, the left will go on tarring Gingrich and his political allies as the grinches who stole Christmas, as "enemies of the poor" and lackeys of the rich. Such witch-hunting is indispensable to the left's intellectual class war. The dehumanization of its opponents is the next best option to developing an argument to refute them.

In fact, there is no conservative party in America. Certainly not Republicans, who are responsible for the major reforms of the Clinton years. The mantle of reaction is better worn by the left, given its resistance to change and its rearguard battles against the market and free trade. But the left controls the culture, and with it the political language. Therefore, in America, reactionaries will continue to be called "progressives" and reformers "conservatives."

6

Ordeal by Slander

W INSTON CHURCHILL ONCE REMARKED that there is nothing more exhilarating than to be shot at without result. Perhaps that is a reason he was a conservative. It guaranteed that he would be shot at him frequently.

I dodged my own political bullet when columnist Jack White smeared me as a racist in *Time*, and I knew I had survived when a favorable review of *Hating Whitey* appeared in the same magazine.

I had hardly begun to enjoy my resurrection, however, when I opened the *New York Times Sunday Magazine* to see myself smeared again as one of a group of conservatives who were on an alleged mission to rehabilitate Joe McCarthy.* After the epithet "racist," "McCarthyite" is probably the label most likely to inflict a mortal wound in our political culture. I was not really surprised that a liberal institution like the *Times* would be the vehicle for such slander. The author had interviewed me for the piece and I was expecting it.

---

* Jacob Weisberg, "The Rehabilitation of Joe McCarthy," *New York Times Sunday Magazine*, November 28, 1999.

Jacob Weisberg's piece, in fact, was almost a carbon copy of an article by Joshua Micah Marshall that had appeared in *The American Prospect* exactly a year before.* Marshall's screed was called "Exhuming McCarthy" and slandered the same small group—Ronald Radosh, Harvey Klehr, John Haynes, Allen Weinstein, and me—labeling us "New McCarthyites." Like Weisberg's piece it failed to provide the slightest evidence for the charge.

The ostensible subject of both articles was a controversy sparked by the efforts of conservative scholars to bring to light new evidence of domestic Communist spying during the Cold War. The evidence had surfaced with the recent release of the "Venona" transcripts and the opening of the Soviet archives. Haynes and Klehr were engaged in a series of groundbreaking studies for Yale University Press based on the documents; Radosh had cowritten the definitive books on the Rosenberg and Amerasia spy cases, and was known to be writing a study of the Spanish Civil War using the new sources; Weinstein is the author of the definitive book on Alger Hiss and had published a book on domestic Communist spies called *The Haunted Wood.* Arthur Herman, a fifth conservative attacked by Weisberg, had just published *Joe McCarthy: Re-examining the Life and Legacy of America's Most Hated Senator*, which also took advantage of the new material. I am not now, nor have I ever claimed to be a scholar in the field of Cold War espionage. I have never written anything about spy cases, have read only those Venona documents contained in secondary studies, and do not intend ever to visit the Soviet archives. What was I doing in Weisberg's piece?

I asked myself this question when Weisberg's article came out and had even put it to the author when he first called me for an

---

*   Following up my observations in the preceding chapter ("The Intellectual Class War"), I will point out that *The American Prospect* is funded by a $5.5 million grant from the Schumann Foundation, an institution headed by Bill Moyers.

interview. At the time, he was hesitant and vague in a way that immediately aroused my suspicions, but then assured me that the article he was writing was "about more than just the controversy," which persuaded me to cooperate. When the article finally appeared, however, it was obvious that Weisberg had lied. My inclusion, I realized, was for the sole purpose of smearing the other four authors—or, more precisely, making the smear of them seem plausible. My usefulness lay in the fact that I am known as a tough moral critic of the left and have made it a point to answer attacks from that quarter in the same uncompromising language as the attacks themselves. The fact that I often write in a polemical in-your-face style rather than a scholarly hedge-your-bet prose promised to provide the necessary evidence for Weisberg's hypotheses.

In preparing his *American Prospect* piece Joshua Micah Marshall had not read enough of my actual work to come up with a "gotcha" quote, but he did introduce me as "the prime example" of someone who "excoriate[s] the entire progressive tradition for the misdeeds of the extreme left." Weisberg (who eventually found a quote) merely varies this description: "Having despised liberals from the left, Horowitz came to hate them just as violently from the right." In other words I was a good candidate to serve as the neo-McCarthyite witch-hunter that would prove Weisberg's case. The employment of this authorial device produced an irony, however, that seems to have escaped both writers. Odd, isn't it, that two men who claim to be horrified at McCarthy's attempts to conflate the innocent with the guilty should lump together three non-ideological scholars (Haynes, Klehr and Weinstein), a social democrat (Radosh), a traditional conservative (Herman), and a conservative libertarian like myself, to accuse them all of rehabilitating McCarthyism?

Weisberg's profile of what he alleges to be my liberalphobia must have puzzled many readers of *Salon* for which I write a biweekly column. Gripped by such demons, why would I choose to write for a magazine run by liberals and leftists, and why would I defend them (as I have) from attacks by the political right? Surely this must be counted strange behavior for an ideologue who is possessed of an undiscriminating hatred of all things left. Why would I have written a defense of Christopher Hitchens*—still a proud tiger of the progressive pack—when he told tales out of school on White House aide Sidney Blumenthal and got a taste of the medicine every radical presumably deserves: betrayal by his leftist friends?

The accounts by Marshall and Weisberg of the controversy over Soviet documents are not merely offenses to the facts, but reversals of the truth. They are expressions of the pair's own ideological project to excoriate the tradition of conservative anticommunism for the misdeeds of an extremist named Joseph McCarthy.

Although Weisberg and Marshall strain bravely to pretend otherwise, the real catalyst of the controversy is the unambiguous lessons of the archival evidence brought to light by the Soviet collapse. The facts revealed inconveniently vindicate the claims of the old anti-Communist right and discredit the partisans of both the Old and New Left who have put up a fierce rearguard action to deny them. Indeed, it is the twenty-year effort by tenured leftists to rehabiltate American Communism that explains not only the heat of the controversy, but why there is a controversy at all. As leftists of the "Third Way," both Weisberg and Marshall appreciate the radioactive nature of the issues for their own political faction. Since their brand of "liberalism" still views McCarthy and his conservative allies as far bigger domestic villains than the Communists, this liberalism is implicated in the behaviors of the left that have now been

---

* "Defending Christopher" in David Horowitz, *Hating Whitey and Other Progressive Causes* (Dallas: Spence Publishing, 1999), 240-48.

exposed. Weisberg and Marshall have simply decided to make the best of a bad situation.

The authors' first task in their defense of the left is to expel the specter the facts have conjured: the internal threat of a subversive left, including the Stalinist left of the early Cold War and its heirs, the anti-Amerika left of the Vietnam era and its politically correct successor in the Clinton years. Today the veterans of these movements dominate the liberal arts faculties of the nation's elite universities and thus the historiography of the Cold War itself. The Weisberg-Marshall strategy is to dismiss the left as "powerless" and "irrelevant." Since such a dismissal also renders irrelevant a reevaluation of the conservative role in containing this threat, the authors' make their next move, which is to demonize conservatives engaged in the present controversy by hanging the albatross of "McCarthyism" around their necks.

As it happens, each of the individuals Marshall and Weisberg have targeted are on record as sharp critics of McCarthy and McCarthyism, specifically his demagoguery and recklessness with the facts, his contempt for the legal process, and his unscrupulous attacks on innocent or half-guilty individuals. Every one of us has also been careful in our writings to credit anti-Communist leftists with their achievements in the battles against domestic totalitarians and to avoid confusing them with the pro-Communist factions of the "progressive" cause. (Weisberg has even less excuse than Marshall for this misrepresentation, since both Radosh and Haynes wrote long letters documenting their anti-McCarthy record in response to Marshall's article.)

While the achievements of anti-Communist liberals and leftists are real, Weisberg necessarily overstates them. For Weisberg, anti-Communist liberals like Arthur Schlesinger and Reinhold Niebuhr represent "the one group that basically got Communism right." But if this is the case, Weisberg cannot explain why the pursuit of domestic spies like Hiss, and of Communist agents like Owen Lattimore, was predominantly—though not exclusively—the work of the anti-Communist right (which included Democrats as well as Republicans). Then as now, the right was the consistent and perdurable champion of the anti-Communist cause. A satisfactory explanation of the dynamics of the internal Cold War would have to explain this fact. Weisberg does not even try.

While Weisberg notes that the anti-Communist liberals he favors have been strangely silent in the current controversy, he does not examine the reason for the silence. Might it have something to do with liberal politics itself? Could the off-again-on-again popular front between liberalism and leftism perhaps explain the paradox? Is there not some truth in the conservative charge that liberals and leftists share goals and differ only in the means to achieve them? On these provocative questions Weisberg takes the Fifth. Instead of confronting them, he diverts the reader's attention by suggesting that the "real" issues in the controversy are psychological, not political.

"Radosh," he writes, "exemplifies a kind of Whig Fallacy in reverse—viewing the present through the lens of one's own painful past." For Weisberg, Radosh's alleged attachment to the melodramas of his youth explains his refusal "to understand ... the way in which Communism, long irrelevant in American politics, has become not just powerless but absurd." (Interestingly, the same issue of the *Times* in which Weisberg's article appears features an op-ed piece entitled "The Next Dialectic," by a best-selling liberal author who writes that Marx "foretold the present cyber-age" and that "writing about globalization in 'Principles of Communism' in 1847, Engels sounds very 1999.")

Of course, Weisberg does not bother to provide evidence for the claim that Radosh is suffering from a case of arrested development (let alone for the assertion that the left lacks influence). Instead, he shifts quite abruptly to me: "Radosh is a mild and temperate critic in comparison with an old friend of his from the New Left, and a fellow red-diaper baby, David Horowitz . . . ."

As Weisberg proceeds with his Horowitz file, it becomes obvious that the sole reason for my appearance in his text, since I am not a historian and played no role in this controversy, is to provide him with the raw material to prove that psychological demons rather than real world concerns drive the anti-Communist side of the debate, distort its analyses, and wildly exaggerate its claims. Since I am the only member of the group to have written an autobiography that is both personal and political, my work offers a unique opportunity: "For those most deeply invested in this universe [of Cold War politics], clinging to anti-Communism is as much a personal as it is a political phenomenon. What comes through vividly in Horowitz's memoirs is a fierce Oedipal struggle entwined with radicalism. Horowitz wanted to antagonize his Communist father; in later years, when he was ailing, Horowitz would bait him by raising the name of Alexander Solzhenitsyn."

When the *Times*'s fact checker read this final sentence to me, I told her that it was such a misrepresentation of what I had written it amounted to a falsehood and that Weisberg might want to reconsider its inclusion. Of course he did not (and could not) change it, because to do so would have destroyed his thesis. Here is the passage from *Radical Son* in which I describe this encounter with my father. It was the mid-1970s, when I was in my thirties and had begun to have second thoughts about the left:

> When our discussions veered into the areas of our political disagreements, I was made to feel the spine of his being. It was as though we were back in the house on 44th Street [twenty years before], arguing over the *Times* again. Yet these new eruptions

were quickly muted by my decision not to press them. I would raise the issue of Solzhenitsyn's new book to see that he had not changed. But when the expected response came, I did not push him to the wall, as I once had. He was too weakened, too beaten for that. When he dismissed Solzhenitsyn as a reactionary doing the Americans' work, I let it pass. Sometimes I would pare down my quest until it was a simple demand for respect . . . What I wanted was my father's recognition that I, too, had won a few hard truths.

In other words, the episode was exactly the opposite of what Weisberg alleges. This passage reveals that, far from seeking to antagonize my father, I felt pain as a frustrated son who wanted to connect with him in an area that was important to us both, and failed. When the failure was undeniable, I backed off. But this mundane filial effort to make contact with an aging parent did not suit Weisberg's purpose, which was to portray me as irreconcilable and my antagonism as a neurosis affecting my entire political perspective. "This sense of acting out of personal injury," Weisberg sums up, "permeates everything Horowitz writes today." What a ruthless way to dismiss an intellectual perspective.

Other misrepresentations follow. Having set up a straw man (the psychologically distressed hater of liberals), Weisberg moves directly to the clinching trope for his political hypothesis: "This explains Horowitz's penchant for depicting Clinton Democrats in terms borrowed from the era of high Stalinism . . . . In the online magazine *Salon*, where he has a column, Horowitz wrote recently, 'It is as though the Rosenbergs had been in the White House, except that the Rosenbergs were little people and naïve.'"

The quote is actually lifted from a column that appeared in a three-part series I wrote for *Salon*, which dealt with the unprecedented breach of America's national security interests during the

Clinton Administration.* This catastrophe is described as the result both of lax security leading to the theft of nuclear weapons by China and the calculated lifting of security controls that allowed the transfer of vital satellite, missile and computer technologies to the Communist dictatorship. Readers of the *Salon* piece will know that the reference to the Rosenbergs was not intended in any way to draw a parallel between Clinton's motives and those of the Communists. I did not invoke the Rosenbergs as an explanation of *why* Clinton allowed these breaches to take place, but as an indication of the magnitude of the loss to American security. When the passage is read in full, it is obvious even to the most obtuse reader that I actually used the analogy to *differentiate* Clinton's actions from the actions of Communists like the Rosenbergs—in other words exactly the opposite of what Weisberg claims:

> It could even be said in behalf of the Rosenbergs that they did not do it for themselves, but out of loyalty to an ideal, however pathetic and misguided. Bill Clinton has no such loyalties— neither to his family, nor his party, nor his country. . . . The wounds he has inflicted on this nation, and every individual within it, with consequences unknown for future generations, cannot be said to have been inflicted for ideological reasons or even out of some perverse dedication to a principle of evil. The destructiveness of Bill Clinton has emerged out of a need that is far more banal—to advance the cause of a self-absorbed and criminal personality.

Christopher Hitchens could have written that.

Weisberg's rancid fantasy is reckless with the facts and destructive of the reputations of those under attack providing an ugly paral-

---

* "The Manchurian President" in David Horowitz, *Hating Whitey and Other Progressive Causes* (Dallas: Spence Publishing, 1999), 273-282.

lel to the author's notorious subject. But it is also anti-intellectual and unhistorical. Weisberg's whole effort is designed to deflect the question that provoked the argument in the first place. Whose view of this epoch was and is correct? Why are there such powerful voices, including the *New York Times*, that are seeking to trivialize this debate and treat it as a mere rehash of dead issues or, worse, as an attempt to resurrect the disreputable politics of the past? The answer to these questions has obvious implications for one's view of both the progressive-liberal tradition and its conservative rival, and hence is hardly irrelevant as Weisberg so disingenuously claims. Indeed, the claim itself is part of the argument.

Discounting the internal Communist threat in the Roosevelt and early Truman years and underrating the external threat in the post-Johnson era have been the hallmarks of modern liberalism and its irregular alliance with the fellow-traveling, pro-Communist left. The summary moment of this strange bedfellowship took place in 1941 when Whittaker Chambers went to Washington to warn the White House that his close aide Alger Hiss was a Communist and a Soviet spy. When the message was conveyed to Roosevelt, the president merely laughed and then elevated Hiss to even higher levels of policy and responsibility. Weisberg's *Times* piece is squarely within this tradition, as is the *Times*'s own treatment of the post-Communist revelations. The *Times*, for example, buried the Venona story when it first broke and has remained skeptical to the bitter end on the question of Hiss's guilt, even as it has continued to cast a sympathetic eye on the anti-American radicals of the Vietnam era.

The liberal temperament reflected in these choices is illustrated by Weisberg's treatment of Owen Lattimore, a figure from this history to whom he makes a passing reference. Lattimore was a famous McCarthy target and—in liberal eyes—a still more famous McCarthy victim. Yet despite all that has been revealed through Venona, the

Soviet archives, and the memoirs of repentant Communists, Weisberg still can describe Lattimore merely as "the China hand absurdly named as the Soviets 'top spy' in the United States."

It is true that this McCarthy claim was false, which is why Wesiberg highlights it. But every conservative scholar in Weisberg's crosshairs has noted this false claim as well, and used it to deplore McCarthy's demagoguery and slander, while remarking on the damage such reckless accusations did to the legitimate anti-Communist cause. Indeed, at the time itself no one was more furious with McCarthy for this overreach than J. Edgar Hoover. To this day, Lattimore has never been proved a spy and nowhere appears as one in the Soviet documents thus far released.

But the image of wounded innocence that surrounded Lattimore then and still does in Weisberg's commentary is even falser to the reality of both the man and the period than the McCarthy smear itself. In fact, the professorial Lattimore was a self-conscious and devious betrayer of his country and a willing servant of the Soviet cause working hand-in-glove with its underground spy apparatus in the United States. As the editor of *Pacific Affairs* and intimate of Lauchlin Currie (the White House *liaison* to the Department of State), Lattimore was one of America's most influential China experts during the Roosevelt and Truman Administrations, a period which marked the crucial stages of the Communist revolution, whose triumph in 1949 preceded McCarthy's crusade by a mere eight months. We now know that Lauchlin Currie, Lattimore's intimate friend and patron at the White House, was a Soviet spy. On Currie's advice, Lattimore hired a KGB collaborator named Michael Greenberg as his assistant at *Pacific Affairs*, and then on his own initiative, hired Chen Han-shen, a Chinese spy, as his coeditor. Lattimore put his request for the coeditor through the channels of the Comintern. Lattimore's own views were pro-Soviet and pro-Mao.

Yet, in the battle with McCarthy, liberals and Democrats (with important exceptions like Arthur Schlesinger) cast Lattimore as the long-suffering hero. Arthur Herman, one of Weisberg's targets, reminds us in his book on McCarthy that Herbert Elliston of the *Baltimore Sun*, Al Friendly of the *Washington Post*, Drew Pearson, I.F. Stone, Eric Sevareid, and Martin Agronsky all supported Lattimore as an idealistic champion of democracy and free speech. The *New York Post* editorialized: "All those who believe in freedom in this country are in the debt of Owen Lattimore." The same political forces painted McCarthy as the devil, while congressional Democrats successfully thwarted his bid to expose Lattimore as the traitor he was.

The release of Soviet documents has allowed us to confirm the following crucial facts about the Cold War battles of this era: (1) The anti-Communist forces of the right were correctly concerned about the internal threat to American security (as were their liberal and socialist allies); (2) The pro-Soviet left was treacherous and subversive; and (3) the Democrats often harbored and protected the Communists who had infiltrated their ranks (their reasons were frequently simply partisan—they were covering up the security failures of the Roosevelt and Truman Administrations).

In obscuring these historical realities, Weisberg and the *Times* are playing a role that parallels the one played by their liberal and fellow-traveling counterparts in the McCarthy era. This includes turning a semiblind eye to the stranglehold exerted by the intellectual heirs of Owen Lattimore—Soviet sympathizers and New Left Marxists—on the teaching of history in American universities. This year, for example, the two main professional historical organizations are headed by an unrepentant former Communist (David Montgomery), and a New Left apologist for the Rosenbergs (Eric Foner). Sympathizers of the old Communist left now dominate both academic fields of Soviet studies and domestic Communism.

The leading academic authority on the McCarthy period, for example, Ellen Schrecker, is a full-blown apologist for American communism. Schrecker's books do not even bother to dream up new defenses for the Communists' treachery, but merely rehash the disingenuous arguments the Communists themselves made at the time. A typical Schreckerism explains that American Communists spied not because they were traitors, but because they "did not subscribe to traditional forms of patriotism."

In discussing Schrecker's work, Weisberg treads lightly over the reality of the left's hold on the historical record. To treat this reality for what it is would require recognizing that conservative scholars have been pushed to the fringes of their profession by a political climate more powerful in excluding dissenters than McCarthy's ever was because its prosecutors are inside the walls of the academy itself. It would mean recognizing that a handful of historians, institutionally marginalized, have struggled courageously to present a balanced view of this past, only to find themselves pilloried as "exhumers of McCarthy." But to acknowledge this would also mean to recognize the power and relevance of the left in the present. It would mean "rehabilitating" the role that ex-Communists like Elizabeth Bentley, conservatives like William F. Buckley, and institutions like the FBI played in the past in defending America against the Communist threat. Instead, Weisberg's plea is that the story of American Communists should be approached "in a less judgmental fashion," as though one can be less judgmental about treason without doing violence to the historical record. His conclusion that even intellectually "the Cold War is history now," indicates that it is a war that "liberals" whose record is ambiguous would prefer to forget. It is more likely that (in Irving Kristol's phrase) the Cold War has merely come home.

For although Weisberg affects to be above the fray, he himself is a partisan in this conflict. Just three years ago, Weisberg wrote a story for *New York* called "The Un-Americans," a peculiar reprise of the McCarthy-era stigma, which he applied to six conservatives featured on the magazine's cover: Phil Gramm, Gordon Liddy, Oliver North, Rush Limbaugh, Pat Robertson, and Jesse Helms. Their collective thought crime was to have criticized the federal government and their subversive "act" to have used words like "revolution" in connection with Gingrich's "Contract with America," and thus—in Weisberg's tendentious indictment—to have provided an ideological rationale for the bombing of a federal building in Oklahoma City that killed 168 people.

When Weisberg called to interview me for his *Times* piece, I brought up the article. I told him I did not trust his ability to treat conservatives like myself fairly, because I remembered this smear. His reply was evasive. He did not remember if he had written such a story, he said. Like the Communists who were questioned about subversion by McCarthy's committee in the 1950s and presented themselves as liberal patriots and defenders of the First Amendment, Weisberg protected himself by pretending not to know what I was talking about.

7

The Army of the Saints

WHILE ORGANIZING A CHARITY EVENT for homeless youngsters, I received a phone message from a liberal friend who was my partner in the effort. She said she had found someone who was willing to volunteer her home for a fundraiser we had planned for the children. Then she paused—"but not if Charlton Heston comes." Another pause. "In fact, none of my friends' homes will be available if Charlton Heston comes." It was unnecessary for her to tell me (as she did under her breath) "they murdered those kids," in order to alert me that this was about the still-fresh Columbine tragedy in Colorado, where two sociopathic teenagers had barged into a high school and ambushed their classmates, killing more than a dozen before turning their weapons on themselves. Nor did she have to connect the dots and say that the passions Charlton Heston provoked stemmed from his position as head of the National Rifle Association (NRA), which had opposed and helped to defeat gun control legislation in the wake of Columbine. This was the cause of her friends' determination to make him a social pariah.

Accustomed as I am to such intolerance in people who otherwise think of themselves as "liberal," this one drew me up short.
Consider, reader, the people you know and call your friends. How
many of them could you name, who would want to bar someone—
let alone a cultural legend—from a social gathering whose sole purpose was to raise money for homeless children? Whom would they
bar? David Duke? O.J. Simpson? Slobodan Milosevic? I do not
think I have a single conservative friend who would say "I will provide my house to help raise money for poor children, but not if Barbra
Streisand comes."

Charlton Heston is no conservative troglodyte. He is a New
Deal Democrat, the former chair of the Hollywood committee for
Martin Luther King's "March on Washington," a lifelong champion
of civil rights and artists' rights, and even a staunch defender of the
National Endowment for the Arts. To those who know him he is a
decent, humane, and ecumenical soul.

Of course, such real world information is entirely irrelevant to
the matter at hand. The hatred liberals obviously bear Heston has
nothing to do with who he is or what he actually believes and feels.
Even Heston's role as spokesman for the NRA fails to make the anti-
Heston passion intelligible to anyone who does not live inside the
ideological bubble that liberals inhabit. Do the three million, mainly
lower middle-class and working-class members of the NRA want to
see children die? Would the legislation they defeated have saved those
children or others to come?

There are twenty thousand gun laws already on the books, seventeen of which were violated by the Columbine killers. What would
one more law accomplish that these twenty thousand could not, especially one what would merely mandate background checks on buy-
ers at gun shows, as the new one did? Is there any evidence, that
these shows are the sites of a significant number of criminal pur-

chases, or that such legislation would have any effect on armed crimes? The Brady Bill—the most celebrated triumph of gun-control advocates in the last decade—has been violated on more than a quarter of a million occasions since its adoption, but the Clinton Administration (although a fierce advocate of the legislation) has only prosecuted a handful of the violators. Is there more than political smoke at issue in this debate?

Or is there any correlation at all between stringent registration laws and reduced gun deaths? A social scientist named John Lott has published a study showing that communities in which citizens are armed have lower incidences of gun violence than communities where guns are relatively absent.* In places like New York, where gun violence has been reduced and the murder rate has been cut by a phenomenal 60 percent, the reason appears to be aggressive police tactics, which have come under fire from many of the same liberals who think gun control is the answer. Do the people who hate Chuck Heston adore New York Mayor Rudy Giuliani? Hardly.

I do not intend this as an argument for or against the gun legislation that was proposed and that failed in the wake of Columbine. It is merely a case for sobriety in assessing the positions of the disputants. The gun legislation proposed after Columbine may or may not have been worthy. But any difference it might make is so insignificant that it could not justify the foam-at-the-mouth response of its proponents or the stigmas they have placed on those, like Heston, who disagree with them about it.

Why are liberals so compulsively intolerant? It is not a question that can be casually dismissed. Conservatives who might shun a Barbra Streisand make no fetish out of "diversity" the way liberals do, nor do they wave the bloody flag of past American witchhunts

---

* John Lott, *More Guns, Less Crime* (Chicago: University of Chicago Press, 1998).

whenever they come under attack, again as liberals notoriously do. Moreover, the little Beverly Hills Inquisition over the possibility that Charlton Heston would materialize at a charity event is no aberrant case of liberal paranoia.

George Stephanopoulos's memories of his days in the White House capture a simliar moment in the command center of the political process. Before impeachment irretrievably tainted the atmosphere of the Clinton White House, Stephanopoulos and the President were discussing an open congressional seat and the prospect of an upcoming special election. "It's Nazi time," Clinton remarked to Stephanopoulos, by which he meant time to get back to campaigning against Republicans. Two years later, at the outset of another campaign, Clinton told Dick Morris. "You have to understand, Bob Dole is *evil*, what he wants is *evil*." This of a war hero who was a consensus builder in his years as Senate majority leader.

Nor is Clinton alone in his rabid hatred of the Republican opposition. Congressman John Lewis, the Democrat from Georgia, publicly referred to House Republicans as "Nazis" merely for proposing to keep the expansion of Medicare within the rate of inflation to save it from bankruptcy. Other Democrats, like Charles Rangel, have referred to Republicans as racists for similar disagreements on budgetary allocations: "Don't you believe that they don't want to dismantle the Social Security system. They are afraid to come out from under their hoods and attack us directly."* (In a variation of the theme, Clinton referred to the Republicans' 1999 proposed across-the-board tax cut as "an assault on women.") As in the case of gun control legislation, there is no perceptible connection between the offenses and the liberal demonization of the offenders.

---

*   Jeff Jacoby, "1998: Another Year of Liberal Slanders," *Boston Globe*, December 31, 1998.

It is not just liberal politicians who harbor extreme views of ordinary conservatives. In the spring 1999 issue of *Dissent* the philosopher Richard Rorty described the Republican House members who thought the president committed perjury and obstruction of justice "greedheads" and "hypocrites of the Christian Right (sometimes known as cultural conservatives)." Only somewhat less overheated was *Dissent* senior editor Paul Berman's description of the same group as "crazed reactionaries." The celebrated law professor Alan Dershowitz went a step further, describing Republican supporters of impeachment as "the forces of evil. Evil. Genuine evil."*

Outside the KKK-Farrakhan hate fringe (which embraces bigots on the left and right), there is no conservative analog to this left-wing paranoia. Conservatives with intellectual credentials comparable to Rorty's—Irving Kristol, Norman Podhoretz, William Buckley, and James Q. Wilson—do not normally (or even rarely) indulge in the kind of ad hominem assualt that seems second nature to Rorty and other left-wing intellectuals when they are writing about their political opponents. As for politicians, perhaps there is a Republican office holder who every now and then enters the electoral cycle with a slanderous war cry (*It's commie time!*), but I certainly haven't met him. There is just no analog to the passion of conservative bashing which has unfairly stained the reputations of figures as disparate as Judge Bork, Justice Thomas, Speaker Gingrich, Representative Barr, and public advocates like Ward Connerly. Conservatives who have not laid a glove on such obvious targets as Barney Frank and Maxine Waters (rhetorical terrorists in their own right), tend to think of their opponents as benighted or irresponsible, or simply misguided, but they do not treat them as agents of the devil as the left generally treats conservatives.

---

* Ibid.

But then Republicans, as we have noted, are political amateurs. They enter politics having left their primary businesses in the private sector, and go to their legislatures to fight city hall over practical matters. They want to restrain the Leviathan that is suffocating enterprise. Or less nobly, they want to harness it to their self-interest. The left has a grander design. Its interest in politics is missionary. It sees government as a redemptive force. It is not there to tinker with gun control laws. It is there, as Hillary Clinton once put it, "to define what it means to be human in the twenty-first century."

The source of leftist intolerance lies in a vision that has roots in the Puritan origins of the American "New World." They see themselves as soldiers in the Army of the Saints—a vision that is incomplete without the archenemy, the Party of Satan. It is the Party of Satan whose minions corrupt the innocent and block the path of human progress. In the fantasies of these liberal Lenins, all the little children killed in drive-by shootings across America could be walking the safe streets of the 'hood, if only the Chuck Hestons of the world would disappear.

8

Tenured Radical

THERE ARE MANY AFRICAN AMERICAN SCHOLARS—Thomas Sowell, Randall Kennedy, Orlando Patterson, Stephen Carter, William Julius Wilson, and Glenn Loury, to name a few—who have made notable contributions to their fields and whose arguments have to be engaged by anyone interested in their subjects. Cornel West, the Alphonse Fletcher Jr. professor at Harvard, is not one of them.

In spite of this—perhaps even because of it—West is a superstar in an academic world that is progressively left and politically correct. He holds dual professorships in theology and African American studies at Harvard and served previously on the faculties of Yale, Princeton, and the University of Paris. His income is probably in the high six figures, and thanks to the academic dominance of his leftist peers, he has received twenty honorary degrees. His public celebrity is such that he was interviewed on the ABC "marathon" to celebrate the millennium by Peter Jennings, who described West as one of the "greatest teachers in America." He receives invitations to to give 150 lectures a year, and his books are required texts in college curricula across the nation.

Only forty-six years old, West has been called "the preeminent African American intellectual of his generation" by Henry Louis Gates and "one of the most authentic brilliant, prophetic and healing voices in America" by Marian Wright Edelman. His work has elicited White House invitations and more requests as a speaker, blurb writer, and distinguished guest than any individual could possibly fill. In a market in which it is increasingly difficult for genuine scholars to get an academic monograph in print, Cornel West has written or edited twenty books that have been published by commercial publishers—sixteen in the last ten years alone.

Given this profusion of titles, however, there is remarkably modest demand for West's work. Except for a thin volume of left-wing boilerplate on current issues entitled *Race Matters*, none of his books appears to have sold in sufficient quantity to justify the commercial support his work has enjoyed. Consulting a publishing industry executive about this mystery, I was told that his books are put into print as "prestige" publications to bring credit to the house, which is as eager to boast a title by an African American professor from Harvard as Harvard is to have an African American professor on its faculty. Now we are being treated to a new *Cornel West Reader*, edited by West himself, which is a publishing attempt to ratify his status as an intellectual force. But the effect of collecting selections from his works is to reveal why West's work has failed to gain intellectual traction outside the academy. His scholarly metier, as this summa reveals, is "prophesy" (by which he means his own). The term exudes pomposity mixed with an aura of vagueness that is characteristic of his entire output. Though his oeuvre combines philosophical grandiosity with postmodern frou-frou, it embarrassingly lacks the intellectual power to sustain either.

The first of West's books was published when he was twenty-nine (and old enough to know better) and was called *Prophesy De-*

liverance! An Afro-American Revolutionary Christianity. Thereafter, he published *Prophetic Fragments, Prophetic Thought in Postmodern Times, Prophetic Reflections, Keeping Faith,* and *Restoring Hope.* If the titles convey a cerebral airiness, the style recalls Jesse Jackson's riffs without the rhymes. "Blather" could have been a term coined with West's ratiocinations in mind. For example, we learn from notes he has supplied for the *Reader* that "prophesy" amounts to combining marxist cliches and religious dogma: "These introductory remarks to my second book, *Prophetic Fragments* (1988), convey my moral outrage at the relative indifference of American religion to the challenge of social justice beyond charity." In other words, he is upset by religion if it is not left-wing politics. An excerpt from *Prophetic Fragments* is even more specific (and an instance of West's typically inflated and clumsy style): "The principal aim of *Prophetic Fragments* is to examine and explore, delineate and demystify, counter and contest the widespread accommodation of American religion to the political and cultural status quo."

A few years ago, Leon Wieseltier wrote a cover feature for *The New Republic* reviewing West's output, entitled "The Decline of the Black Intellectual." West's productions were, in Wieseltier's mortifying description, "monuments to the devastation of a mind by the squalls of theory." Surveying the entire corpus of West's academic work, Wieseltier found him to be an intellectual empty suit whose writing was "noisy, tedious, slippery . . . sectarian, humorless, pedantic and self-endeared." He judged West's works to be "almost completely worthless." As Gertrude Stein once said of the city of Oakland, there was no "there" there.

Ironically, it is the very incoherence of West's intellectual persona that he has been able to turn into a virtue. One of the early catalysts of his rise to prominence was his lonely plea for racial harmony at time of particularly ugly interracial attacks. Louis Farrakhan was denouncing Judaism as a "gutter religion," Jesse Jackson was referring to New York as "hymietown," and black "separatism" was becoming a fashionable posture on the political left. As a black Christian Marxist, West was almost alone in declaring that it might not be appropriate for black militants to hate all whites and Jews. By the standards of the contemporary academy, this made him both ethnically perfect and politically correct.

Having been elevated to the Harvard empyrean, however, West was in danger of losing touch with his "roots." So he reached out in the opposite direction as well. Among other significant gestures, he endorsed *Race Traitor*—an academic magazine that calls for the "abolition of whiteness"—as "the most visionary, courageous journal in America," and he has embraced two of America's most notorious race haters and anti-Semites.

Thus, the most prominent black radical to preach ecumenical healing between blacks and Jews is also a friend to Louis Farrakhan, the most influential racist and anti-Semite in America. As presidential candidate Bill Bradley's adviser on African American issues, West encouraged the Senator to meet with Al Sharpton (whose own candidacy for the Senate West had supported). This was the same Sharpton who had railed against "diamond merchants" after a black mob lynched the Hasidic Jew Yankel Rosenbaum in Crown Heights and who, in an effort to drive a Jewish-owned store out of Harlem, incited his black followers against the "white interloper." (A deranged arsonist in Sharpton's organization eventually torched the store and killed seven people.) West can maintain this contradictory position— racial healer and bedfellow of racial extremists—because, in the end, no one takes his radicalism seriously. He can wave the bloody shirt to manipulate the guilt of white liberals while acting the gentleman host at the Harvard faculty club.

The *Cornel West Reader* reads like the diary of a Jamesean

ingénue—breathless with discoveries both real and imagined—particularly the discovery of self: "I am a Chekhovian Christian." This is West's announcement—blunt and incomprehensible—of his intellectual identity. In the introduction to his *Reader*, West makes many references to this "Chekhovian Christian viewpoint," but looking for an explanation of what this—or any other concept embedded in West's meandering syntax—might mean is futile, a bit like looking for a breath of fresh air at the bottom of the sea. In the end, West's self-identified perspective seems to be no more substantive than the tedious injection of yet more religious sentiment into marxist cant: "I am a Chekhovian Christian . . . . By this I mean that I am obsessed with confronting the pervasive evil of unjustified suffering and unnecessary social misery."

If we ask why "Chekhov" (and not, say, Tony Kushner or Spike Lee), all we get is a blast of hot air: "I find the incomparable works of Anton Chekhov—the best singular body by a modern artist. . . . [Chekhov's] magisterial depiction of the cold Cosmos, indifferent Nature, crushing Fate and the cruel histories that circumscribe desperate, bored, confused and anxiety-ridden yet love-hungry people, who try to endure against all odds, rings true to me." But what does this have to do with Chekovianism as a genus of Christianity? It is simply beyond West to address the question his juxtaposition of Chekhov and Christianity begs: how can a Christian universe informed by love and the prospect of redemption be squared with his cold Chekovian cosmos, an "indifferent Nature [and] crushing Fate?" It would not pay to spend too much time answering that one.

Throughout West's work its superficiality is relentlessly and embarrassingly accompanied by intellectual status-seeking that is worthy of a character in Moliere: "Despite my Chekovian Christian conception of what it means to be human—a view that invokes premodern biblical narratives . . . I stand in the skeptical Christian tradition of Montaigne, Pascal and Kierkegaard." "My Chekovian Christian viewpoint is idiosyncratic and iconoclastic. My sense of the absurdity and incongruity of the world is closer to the Gnosticism of Valentinus, Luria or Monoimos." "My intellectual lineage goes more through Schopenhauer, Tolstoy, Rilke, Melville, Lorca, Kafka, Celan, Beckett, Soyinka, O'Neill, Kazantzakis, Morrison and above all, Chekhov . . . . And, I should add, it reaches its highest expression in Brahms's *Requiem* and Coltrane's 'A Love Supreme.'"

What can one say of such blathering conceit? But notwithstanding the intellectual jive talk, comedy is finally an inapt term to describe a yearning like West's. For his intellectual charade reflects the political malaise of the modern academy, which has abandoned its traditional role as an institution "dedicated to the disinterested pursuit of knowledge" to assume a new role as an "agency of social change." West's career is a product of the new political university, his plight that of a paradigmatic affirmative-action baby, whom the good wishes of his enlightened oppressors have elevated so far above his merits that he has lost sight of terra firma below. As a result, West has been condemned to an intellectual life of suspended animation, his entire being addressed to the impossible task of proving that he is someone he can never be.

Although almost incapable of writing a concrete sentence, West shows just enough autobiographical leg in his new book to betray the sources of this dilemma. Growing up as a precocious black child in the radical 1960s, the young West became a black militant activist, president of his senior high school class, and thus inevitably a target of liberal uplift. At seventeen, he was recruited to Harvard where his political militancy convinced him that he had more to tell his professors than they had to teach him. As he informs us without the least self-irony, he was determined as an incoming freshman at Harvard to press the university and its intellectual traditions into the service of his political agendas. It seems not to have occurred to him that, as a venerable educational institution, perhaps Harvard should impress itself on him. "Owing to my family, church, and the black social movements of the 1960s, I arrived at Harvard unashamed of my African, Christian, and militant de-colonized outlooks. More pointedly, I acknowledged and accented the empowerment of my black styles, mannerisms and viewpoints, my Christian values of service, love, humility, and struggle, and my anti-colonial sense of self-determination for oppressed people and nations around the world." This is the authentic voice of 1960s left wing arrogance.

West's entry into Harvard was a crucial rite of passage for what might have been a promising young student: the confrontation between a brash but impressionable youth and a three-hundred-year-old educational institution dedicated to passing on the intellectual traditions of a three-thousand-year-old culture. It was a system that had shaped generations of bright and brash young men before him. Yet it was a system that failed Cornel West, for it was a moment in which Harvard's own cultural ramparts, undermined by the cultural radicalism of the age, were collapsing before militancy like his.

In the years Cornel West was a student at Harvard, traditional disciplines were being broken down, intellectual authority assaulted, and the liberal arts university transformed into a political club. The old and tested rules of scholarship were summarily rejected. New disciplines and even entire institutions were created—ideologically committed Black Studies and Women's Studies Departments and paganized theology schools. Marxist and postmarxist curricula replaced the traditional teaching of English literature and other humanities.

Along with the new academic dispensation came a new intellectual attitude towards ignorance especially if it came in blackface or any other mask of the designated oppressed. Instead of educating and disciplining their politically aggressive intellectual tyro, Harvard and its liberal faculties merely encouraged him. It was the politically correct thing to do.

The abortive education of Cornel West is a classic case of what Shelby Steele has astutely analyzed as the encounter of liberal whites looking for moral absolution and radical blacks looking for the easy way up.* And who could blame them or Cornel West for taking advantage of the situation? As a result, this once promising student never learned the difference between an intellectual argument and a political attitude, between the pursuit of an intellectual inquiry, and the search for "answers" that were ideologically correct. The *Cornel West Reader* is a testament to the intellectual vacuum that a progressive education creates. The trappings of intellect are in place, the canonical names invoked, the capsule histories recalled, the theories broadly rehearsed. But behind the footnotes and the latinate phrases, the vulgar activist mind remains feverishly at work. A "discourse" is produced in which political postures relentlessly substitute for serious thought.

The intellectual ruin of Cornel West is not an isolated case. There is a whole generation of racially favored intellectual waterflies—bell hooks, Eric Michael Dyson, Robin D. G. Kelley, Patricia Williams, to name a few—who have been encouraged because of their political aptitude and whose cultural elevation is not only unrelated to any serious intellectual achievement, but has eliminated the possibility of one. For them, as for Cornel West, the pathos lies in what might have been. The left-wing university culture has stripped them of an educational opportunity that is given only once in a lifetime. Meanwhile, the self-appointed social redeemers of the tenured elite, whom West thanks in his acknowledgements for helping him along, are in

---

* Shelby Steele, *A Dream Deferred* (New York: HarperCollins, 1998).

reality the very people who deprived him of a chance to learn the old-fashioned way, and thus helped to destroy whatever intellectual potential he may once have had.

AFTERWORD

This chapter first appeared as a column in *Salon* magazine. After its publication I was attacked by several leftists for "obsessing" on black leaders and black intellectuals. Tavis Smiley, the author of *Hard Left* and host of a prominent talk show on Black Entertainment Television, called my profile of West "reprehensible"—though without explaining why. Politicallyblack.com, an atrociously edited left-wing e-zine, accused me of building "a career upon being an authority on a subject where [my] credentials are suspect," that is, "race matters." Though I have written more than a dozen books only one is about race—and only a third of that text (*Hating Whitey*) actually addresses the issue. These attacks are merely an attempt to embargo any discussion by anybody of the intellectual charlatanism and moral hypocrisy rampant these days in the left.

My criticism of Cornel West is not for his having risen, as an African American, to a place beyond his desert. There are plenty of mediocrities—both white and "of color," both male and female— who have managed to collect big checks in our imperfect social order. Nor am I especially outraged at West's hypocrisy in putting on marxist airs when he himself is in the top 2- or 5-percent income bracket that he regularly accuses of sucking up the wealth in America at the expense of the bottom half. Marxist claptrap, after all, is an occupational hazard of today's academic environment. Nor do I especially seek to "out" him for the mendacity with which he presents himself in jive-humble as a "brother off the block," when he is in fact a scion of college graduates and a son of middle class privilege.

What I do have a problem with is the self-righteousness in a career that feeds off the suffering of those poor African Americans who were the intended beneficiaries of affirmative action, but whose places pretenders like West have usurped. Promoting himself as a man concerned with social justice is the ultimate irony in the odyssey of a protomillionaire, whose wealth derives from the selling of snake-oil concoctions, in particular those crackpot leftist ideologies whose legacy is a bankrupt welfare system, a race-based social perspective, and a politicized academy that sends crippling messages to the poor, the disdvantaged, and the simply left behind. To preen oneself on having a social conscience on the basis of such achievements is truly an outrage, and I make no apologies for pointing this out.

9

Constructing Reality

THE FINAL YEAR OF THE MILLENNIUM was a bad one for pre-varicators of the political left. First it was Nobel laureate and Guatemalan terrorist Rigoberta Menchu who was ex-posed by fellow leftist David Stoll as a self-fabricating poseur. Then it was feminist icon and self-proclaimed suburban housewife Betty Friedan unmasked (again by a political comrade) as a longtime pro-pagandist for the Stalinist left and a first-degree political fibber.* Then it was the turn of Modern Language Association president and PLO apologist Edward Said to have his inventions unmasked, revealing him to be a cunning purveyor of biographical myth. These creative dissemblers did not conceive their deceptive constructions of self in isolation. Instead, they were crafted, in each case, to serve a radical cause. Thus they form part of an intellectual continuum with what Leon Trotsky once termed the "Stalin school of falsifica-

---

* See David Horowitz, "I, Rigoberta Menchu, Liar" and "Feminist Fibber" in *Hating Whitey and Other Progressive Causes* (Dallas: Spence Publishing, 1999), 165-73, 225-31.

tion" in which historical data are tortured in the interests of a politically useful "truth."

Rigoberta Menchu presented herself as a poor, uneducated Mayan peasant whose Guatemalan family had been deprived of its land by a *ladino* ruling class descended from the European conquerors of her indigenous people. Rigoberta's story told how the oppressors destroyed her family when they peacefully petititioned to regain the land that had been taken. According to Rigoberta, hers was not an individual tragedy but "the story of all poor Guatemalans." In her telling, autobiography became political parable. Any morally decent reader would be persuaded of the justice of the cause of the urban revolutionaries whose spokesperson she had become and whose strategy was to foment violent confrontations in the Guatemalan countryside.

Every salient element of Rigoberta's parable, however, was based on a biographical lie. She was neither poor nor uneducated. Her family had not been dispossessed by a *ladino* ruling class but by Mayans—in fact by members of the Menchu family itself. The violence they suffered was not unprovoked, but was the consequence of retaliations for the violence initiated by the terrorists whose pawn she had become.

In *The Feminine Mystique*, a book that launched modern feminism, Betty Friedan presented herself as a suburban housewife who had never given a thought to "the woman question," until a few years before. According to her, the catalyst for her new awareness was a Smith College reunion where she encountered the dissatisfactions of her well-educated female classmates unable to balance traditional roles with modern careers. There were many views Friedan could have taken of the data she subsequently collected from the women she interviewed. An unparallelled technological revolution was unfolding in America whose consequences included the dramatic easing of household chores and the even more dramatic liberation from life-threatening conditions associated with childbirth and sex. All this provided women with options for new social roles, and for entry into workplaces and professions where few had previously ventured.

The sheer suddenness of the change, along with the attendant problems inherent in such a transformation, would have been disorienting for any group. But Friedan chose to view the malaise she witnessed in political terms—not as the ambiguities of an epic transition, but as the effects of a male conspiracy to oppress females and confine them to traditional roles. In Friedan's radical melodrama, middle class marriage became a "comfortable concentration camp," men's traditionally protective attitudes towards women the oppressive stance of a master race.

It has now been revealed that Betty Friedan was not very candid about the facts of her own life or the sources of her radical perspective. She was hardly a suburban housewife when she wrote *The Feminine Mystique*, but a veteran of twenty-five years of professional journalism in the communist left. It was in the political left that she was indoctrinated in the politics of "the woman question" and the idea that women in America were "oppressed." Friedan's own life belied the portrait she drew. Even before she wrote *The Feminine Mystique*, whose writing her husband supported, she had a full-time writing and research career as a professional ideologue. She lived in a Hudson River mansion, where she also had a full-time maid to care for her children and relieve her of household duties. But she and her supporters suppressed these facts for nearly half a century because they were inconvenient for the persona and the theory she was determined to promote.

Like Rigoberta Menchu and Betty Friedan, Edward Said is a postmodern dissembler intent on distorting the facts of his life for political ends. For thirty years, in autobiographical writings and published interviews and even a film for the BBC, he presented himself as a Palestinian Everyman. In all of these he shaped his personal story as a case study of the criminal dispossession that he claimed Israel had committed against his Arab people. To be sure, Said was a wealthy Everyman, a member of the Palestinian cultural and monied elite. But in his artful hands that very fact only served to emphasize the plight of the poorest Palestinians. Reviewing one of Said's many books on this subject, Salman Rushdie observed that by writing about his "internal struggle: the anguish of living with displacement, with exile," Said "enables us to feel the pain of his people."*

According to the official biography Said constructed and then retailed until his unmasking, he was born in 1935 in Jerusalem and grew up in a house located at 10 Brenner Street in the Talbiyeh district. He lived there until the moment in 1948 when Jewish occupiers dispossessed his family and Israel became a state. If Said did not state this in so many words, he constructed his references to his early life in ways that compelled readers to conclude as much. "I was born in Jerusalem and spent most of my formative years there and, after 1948, when my entire family became refugees, in Egypt." But the house on Brenner Street, it is now revealed, did not belong to Said's parents, but to his aunt and uncle, nor did he spend "most of [his] formative years there," as he claimed.*

Said's political uses of memory, and particularly of the memories surrounding the house at 10 Brenner Street, were on display in a speech he gave in 1998 at Birzeit University on the West Bank. "The house from which my family departed in 1948—was displaced—was also the house in which the great Jewish philosopher Martin Buber lived for a while, and Buber of course was a great apostle of coexist-

---

* Salman Rushdie, "Between Worlds: Edward Said Makes Sense of His Life," *London Review of Books*, May 7, 1998.

ence between Arabs and Jews, but he didn't mind living in an Arab house whose inhabitants had been displaced." In other words, in Said's version of the past, even Martin Buber, the most prominent Jewish critic of a specifically "Jewish" state, who had proposed instead a binational entity that would be both Jewish and Arab, actively participated in the dispossession of the Arab population. Such hypocrites, these Jews.

Except that it was Said's aunt and uncle who evicted Buber and not the other way around. The eviction took place in 1942. Buber had been living there as a refugee from Nazi Germany, which he had left with his wife and two teenage granddaughters in 1938. The fact that the Bubers would have been killed had they not been able to find refuge in Jerusalem apparently meant nothing to the Saids when it came to terminating their lease, nor to Edward in weighing the Jewish presence in a country that was never his "home."

In 1924, the Balfour Declaration allowed the possibility of a Jewish presence in the British Mandate in Palestine. It is an event that in Said's telling marks the beginning of the criminal dispossession of his family and people. In that year, however, the Saids were not in Palestine, but living halfway across the world, as American citizens in Boston, where they had landed in 1911. This was not atypical of the Palestinian elite itself, which, by most historical accounts, had no strong sense of national identity, let alone a nationalist grievance, until thirty years later, after the establishment of the Jewish state. The Palestine Liberation Organization itself was not created until 1954—six years after the creation of Israel. Indeed, when the Saids left America in 1926, it was not to emigrate to a "homeland" in Palestine but to Cairo, where they became Egyptian citizens and established a prosperous business. Not once in the ensuing twenty years before the emergence of Israel did the Saids think to resettle in the land called Palestine. Egypt was their home.

The myth Edward Said has so artfully fabricated plays well on liberal guilt, but wreaks havoc with the facts. The United Nations partitioned Palestine in 1947, leaving well-defined sectors for both Arabs and Jews, but the Palestinian Arabs rejected the partition. A coalition of the surrounding Arab states then attacked the Jews and attempted to drive them into the sea. The destruction of Israel is the official agenda of the Palestinian cause, and of Edward Said, to this very day. Said opposes the current Oslo peace process and is politically further to the left of Yassir Arafat than Benjamin Netanyahu is to the right of Shimon Peres and Ehud Barak. What he seeks to accomplish through his fabrication of self is the presentation of Palestinian extremism as political moderation, the simple reflex of a humanitarian conscience.

The facts of Said's life have been retrieved from these false memories by a Jewish scholar and lawyer named Justus Weiner, who spent three years researching the historical record, and published his findings in *Commentary* in the Fall of 1999.* Weiner's attempts to interview Said's relatives and friends alerted Said to the investigation, and he responded with an autobiography published a month later under the title *Out of Place*.

Having been caught in his own fictional web, Said constructed his biography to accord more closely with the facts Weiner was certain to reveal. In the new text, the Egyptian childhood is duly restored. But *Out of Place* is no less a deception, since the text does not mention the false impression the author had promoted for thirty years. Moreover, far from conceding that an admission was in order, Said replied to Weiner's article with shrill character attacks. His opening salvo appeared in the Arab press under the headline: "Defa-

---

* Justus Weiner, "'My Beautiful Old House' and Other Fabrications by Edward Said," *Commentary*, September 1999, 23-31.

mation, Zionist Style": "Given the approach of the final status negotiations between Israel and the Palestinians, it seems worthwhile
to record here the lengths to which right-wing Zionists will go to
further their claims on all of Palestine against those of the country's
native Palestinian inhabitants who were dispossessed as an entire
nation in 1948."

Said's attempt to link Weiner's article about his misrepresentations to a "Zionist" agenda could hardly have been more cynical since
Said himself opposed the negotiations as a "sellout," while Weiner
did not even mention them in his article. Said's reference to the
Palestinian dispossession could not have been more loaded, ignor-
ing as it did the fact that the Palestinians were the aggressors and
their agenda was truly an ethnic cleansing (as the Jews' was not).
Moreover, he ignored that the terrible consequences of the aggression were felt on both sides. For while it was true that hundreds of
thousands of native Palestinians were driven into Arab lands in 1948,
it was also true that hundreds of thousands of Jews were driven out
of Arab countries. They were also forced to leave the West Bank
and eastern Jerusalem, as well as the Old City, which is the holiest
place on earth for Jews. Reasonable people might conclude that this
fateful episode encompassed two national tragedies, but not Edward
Said.

Nor was he contrite about his falsification of personal details.
Taking the same tack as Rigoberta Menchu, who claimed—after
she was exposed—that her fabrications were a Mayan cultural tradition in which it was allegedly common to conflate many people's
biographies with one's own, Said tried to hide behind the Arab understanding of "family" as an extended clan: "[Weiner] does not realize . . . that the family house was in fact a family house in the Arab
sense, which meant our families were one in ownership. . . . I have
never claimed to have been made a refugee, but rather that my ex-

tended family, all of it—uncles, cousins, aunts, grandparents—in fact was. By the spring of 1948, not a single relative of mine was left in Palestine, ethnically cleansed by Zionist forces."

But this is simply false. The names of Said's parents were not on the deed to the "family house" at 10 Brenner Street. Moreover, just last March, in an interview with an Arab paper, Said lamented: "I feel even more depressed when I remember my beautiful old house surrounded by pine and orange trees in Al-Talbiyeh in east [actually west] Jerusalem which has been turned into a 'Christian embassy.'" No cultural ambiguity here. Of course, as an American and a linguist, Said would have known very well the meaning his audience would attribute to the words he used in thirty years of constructing his political deception.

We are presented, then, with three major figures of left-wing movements caught in the fabrication not only of their personal histories but of history itself. Are their attempted constructions of reality mere coincidence, or is there a deeper lesson to be learned from these episodes? Over and over again, the world vision of the left has failed in this century not because the ideas behind it were not seductively noble, but because they did not work. The vision of the left is by nature a romance of good and evil, of liberators and oppressors. Is the requirement of sustaining so Manichean a vision the flattening of a more complex reality by reshaping it? Is the vision itself so at odds with the reality that it necessitates this lying, and requires an underpinning of fiction to sustain its romance? More practical and prosaic minds will conclude that there is.

10

Still No Regrets

W HAT KIND OF PERSON, having been associated with a gang that carried out an execution-style murder of an African American educator and killed an innocent woman bystander during a robbery, could still, when finally arrested for an attempted assassination, be championed as a well-meaning "idealist" by church officials, Democratic Party legislators, liberal columnists, and local activist groups concerned with civil rights and the environment? The answer is: a progressive activist who has remained faithful to her leftist faith.

Twenty-five years ago, Kathleen Soliah went underground as a fugitive. She was wanted by police as a suspect in the planting of pipe bombs under two randomly selected police cars. The bombs were powerful enough to have killed the occupants had they not failed to explode. Soliah was a member of the Symbionese Liberation Army (SLA), a group led by a black ex-convict Donald DeFreeze who took the nom de guerre "Cinqué" after the slave who led the revolt aboard the *Amistad*. The group of a dozen or so terrorists and their supporters appeared suddenly in the early 1970s. Their defining slogan was "Death to the fascist insect that preys on the life of the people."

After a series of kidnappings and killings, DeFreeze and five other SLA members were cornered by police in a house in Los Angeles and killed in the shootout when they failed to surrender. Soliah led a rally for the "victims" in Berkeley's "Ho Chi Minh Park" claiming that the six outlaws had been "viciously attacked and murdered by five hundred pigs in L.A." Soliah singled out her best friend Angela Atwood, one of the dead SLA members, saying: "I know she lived happy and she died happy. And in that sense, I'm so very proud of her."

Soliah was apprehended in St. Paul, Minnesota, on June 16, 1999. She had been living for more than twenty years as a fugitive under the pseudonym "Sara Jane Olson" and had married a doctor named Fred Peterson. Within a week of her arrest, 250 sympathizers and friends had raised one million dollars in bail to secure her release. The *Minneapolis Star-Tribune* described the attitude of the liberal community in St. Paul after learning of Olson-Soliah's past in these terms: "In the days since her June 16 arrest, Olson has been almost canonized: reader of newspapers for the blind, volunteer among victims of torture, organizer of soup kitchens. The office manager of the Minnehaha United Methodist Church, where she is a member of the congregation, called on its members to build a "contingent of support." Twenty of them were said to have been in court in California on the day she was arraigned.

Soliah's brother-in-law Michael Bortin was a Berkeley radical and also an SLA member, as was his wife Josephine, Soliah's sister. (Soliah's brother was also in the SLA.) Interviewed by reporters, Bortin attempted to explain the relationship between the radical gangster Soliah and the St. Paul housewife Sara Jane Olson, who was such an upstanding member and loved member of the progressive community: "There's not this dichotomy between what Kathy was and what she is now. She was doing the same things in the early 1970s." There is more truth in that statement than in a dozen books on the New Left by tenured radicals. Bortin claimed that it was the assassinations of Kennedy and Martin Luther King, the presidency of Richard Nixon, and the war in Vietnam that changed the attitudes of the Soliahs to make them SLA members. "We lost our faith in the country, in due process. In law and justice."

Maybe so. Back then, I was one of the editors of *Ramparts*, the largest publication of the New Left. Like Bortin and Soliah, I would have described myself then as a "revolutionary" who had "lost faith in my country." But along with many other leftists at the time (and unlike Bortin and the Soliahs), I had not lost my mind. Nor had I lost my sense of decency completely. After the SLA committed its first heinous acts, I wrote an editorial for *Ramparts* condemning them as a criminal mob. It was the first editorial for *Ramparts* that I wrote that I did not sign. I was impressed enough by their actions to be concerned that they might come and kill me.

The SLA announced itself to the world on November 6, 1973, in a gruesome deed that went all but unmentioned in the reportage on Soliah's arrest. Without giving any warning, three SLA soldiers ambushed and gunned down the first African American superintendent of schools in Oakland. Dr. Marcus Foster, a father of three, was met with a hail of bullets when he stepped into the parking lot behind the Oakland School District office on his way home. The bullets had been tipped with cyanide, so he would have no chance. His crime, according to the SLA's official death warrant was not that he sided with the rich, as the few press reports that even mentioned his death have claimed, but that he followed a directive from the school board to issue identification cards to students. The cards were designed to protect students from the intrusion of drug dealers and gang members who had been wandering onto their campuses with intent to do them harm.

The Foster killing revolted me, as it did many but not all members of the radical community. *Ramparts* received several letters like one by Yippee leader Stew Albert, accusing us of "giving a green light" to the police to hunt down and "murder" the SLA warriors. Leonard Weinglass, lawyer for Tom Hayden, Abbie Hoffman, and the Chicago Seven and later counsel for Black Panther cop-killer Mumia Abu Jamal, represented the families of the dead SLA members and sought monetary restitution from the city of Los Angeles. Weinglass claimed that the Los Angeles police had denied his clients justice. In my view, justice had been done. If anything, the SLA killers hadn't been punished enough.

In fairness to Soliah, it is not clear that she was aware of the SLA's intentions prior to the murder of Foster, although she certainly embraced them afterwards. According to Patty Hearst, who was kidnapped by the SLA and then converted to their cause, Soliah participated in a 1975 bank robbery the SLA committed in a Sacramento suburb. An innocent bystander, Myrna Lee Opshal, who had come to the bank to deposit church funds, was "accidentally" shot and killed by SLA member Emily Harris. Later, Harris dismissed the killing to her comrades saying the victim was "a pig" because "she was married to a doctor."

These were the deeds, and this was the mentality, of the gang to which Kathleen Soliah dedicated her radical political life. Now she is once again being defended by progressives, who encouraged the SLA then and who continue to blame the Vietnam War and Richard Nixon for whatever evils they themselves have done. But if Kathy Soliah's crimes are excused by her enemy, Nixon, why would not Nixon's be excused by the crimes *his* enemies—the Communists—committed?

Soliah's attorney Stuart Hanlon is a veteran of the William Kunstler-Leonard Weinglass school of radical alibis, and thus well-suited to defend her. He recently helped Johnnie Cochran get a pass for convicted murderer and former Black Panther Geronimo Pratt by falsely claiming the FBI and police had conspired to frame Pratt because of his passion for "social justice."*

The radical fantasy that turned the Soliahs into paranoid conspirators is very much alive today in the rhetoric of the left, which is unrelenting in its insane depiction of America as a repressive, racist, sexist empire. It has been kept alive by the radical rewriting of the history of the 1960s in which "noble idealists" like Soliah are portrayed as having declared war on government "fascists" and "imperialists." Consequently, whatever bad deeds they committed, they always are remembered as the innocent victims of the greater evil of those they opposed.

A library of memoirs by aging New Leftists and "progressive" academics recalls the rebellions of the 1960s. But hardly a page in any of them has the basic honesty—or sheer decency—to say "Yes, we supported these murderers and those spies, and the agents of that evil empire," or to say so without an alibi. I would like to hear even one of these advocates of "social justice" make this simple acknowledgment: "We greatly exaggerated the sins of America and underestimated its virtues, and we're sorry." I would like to hear that from Soliah and her apologists. I would like to hear them pay a moment's tribute to Marcus Foster and to Myrna Opshal, and to the brave policemen and FBI agents who risked their lives to protect other Americans, including progressives, from the harm these criminals intended. I would like to hear them say, just once, "I'm sorry."

---

* See David Horowitz, "Johnnie's Other O.J.," in *Hating Whitey and Other Progressive Causes* (Dallas: Spence Publishing, 1999), 123-37.

V

LAST WORDS

I I

A Letter from the Past

TWENTY-FIVE YEARS AGO, on December 13, 1974, my friend
Betty Van Patter disappeared from a tavern called the Berkeley Square and was never seen alive again.

Six months earlier, I had recruited Betty to keep the books of
the Educational Opportunities Corporation, an entity I had created
to run a school for the children of the Black Panther Party. Subsequently she became the bookkeeper for the Black Panther Party itself. It was probably because she was asking too many questions
about the Panthers' illegal activities that they decided to kill her. On
January 17, 1975, the police fished her battered corpse out of the waters of San Francisco Bay.

At the time, the Panthers were still being defended by writers
like Murray Kempton and Garry Wills in the pages of the *New York
Times* and by soon-to-be Governor Jerry Brown. Jerry Brown was a
political confidant of Elaine Brown who had hired Betty and whom
Huey Newton had appointed to stand in for him as the Panther
leader while he was in "exile" in Cuba. Ten years later, at a bizarre
meeting in his home in Oakland, Huey Newton told me "Elaine

killed Betty." But I realized in that instant that he had given the order himself from Cuba.

At the time of Betty's death, Elaine was riding a wave of public approval. She was running for Oakland City Council and had just secured a quarter-of-a-million-dollar grant from the Nixon Administration under a federal juvenile delinquency program. J. Anthony Kline, the consigliere to whom she had been able to turn when the party's enforcers got in trouble with the law, was about to be named to Governor Brown's cabinet where his job was to appoint every new superior court judge in California. (Today he is a justice on the First Circuit Court of Appeals in San Francisco).

In pursuit of answers to the mystery of Betty's death, I subsequently discovered that in the course of conducting extortion, prostitution, and drug rackets in the Oakland ghetto the Panthers had killed more than a dozen people. While these criminal activities were taking place, the Panthers enjoyed the support of the American left, the Democratic Party, the Bay Area Trades Union Council, and even the Oakland business establishment. The head of the Clorox Corporation, Oakland's largest company, for example, sat on the board of the Educational Opportunities Corporation.

On a far smaller scale, the Panther killings were an American version of the "Katyn massacre," the infamous murder of Polish officers carried out on Stalin's orders that the left denied and kept hidden for decades, until the opening of the Soviet archives. The totalitarian nature of the Soviet state made it relatively easy to understand how the information that would settle the case could be kept hidden for years. It was much harder for me to understand why in democratic America the Panthers should be able to get away with these murders and why the nation's press should turn a blind eye to a group that law enforcement had properly made an object of its attentions.

Whatever the reasons, the fact remains that to this day not a single organization of the mainstream press has ever investigated the Panther murders. This includes *Sixty Minutes*, whose chief investigative producer, Lowell Bergman, was a member of the Berkeley left, knew Betty and her daughter personally, and was familiar with the facts of the case. This media silence continues even though the story is one that touches the lives and political careers of the entire liberal establishment, including the first lady and the deputy attorney general in charge of civil rights for the Clinton Administration. Both Hillary Clinton and Bill Lanh Lee began their political careers as law students at Yale by organizing demonstrations in 1970 to shut down the university and stop the trial of seven Panther leaders accused of ordering the torture and execution of a black youth named Alex Rackley.

This silence is even more puzzling since the details of the story have managed to trickle out over the years as the result of efforts by myself and my colleague Peter Collier; by journalists Kate Coleman, Ken Kelley, and Hugh Pearson; and one or two others including most particularly David Talbot and David Weir, respectively the editor and managing editor of *Salon* magazine. Because of these efforts, informed citizens are at least aware of the murders. On the other hand, unlike in the Soviet Union, where testimonies emerged as soon as the threat of retaliation was gone, in twenty-five years few additional witnesses have come forward to add to our knowledge about these American crimes.

Many former Panthers are still intimidated by the threat of possible reprisals from Panther leaders who have committed crimes on which the statute of limitations has not run out. But there are hundreds if not thousands of white radical veterans of the 1960s who have some knowledge of these deeds and little to fear, but who have chosen to remain silent and complicit to this day. These include notable figures like Tom Hayden, lawyers like Gerald Lefcourt, and journalists like *Los Angeles Times* columnist Robert Scheer, who defended and promoted the Panthers as revolutionary heroes at the time and have failed to correct that impression ever since. But it also includes many lesser figures who worked day in and day out to facilitate the Panthers rise to power and to coverup their crimes along the way. Evidently, they have remained convinced that even though these crimes were committed, they were not. Or perhaps that if these crimes were indeed committed, it is (and was) no responsibility of theirs, and for political reasons best left unexamined.

I am constantly asked by people who have read my autobiography *Radical Son* or who have heard me talk about these events how it is possible for my former comrades on the left to remain so stubbornly devoted to "experiments" that have failed, to doctrines that are false, and to causes that are demonstrably wrongheaded and even evil. On November 20, 1999, just three weeks before the anniversary of Betty's disappearance, an answer to these questions came in the form of a letter from an old friend whom I had not heard from in fifteen years. The sender of the letter was Art Goldberg, a radical journalist who had been deeply involved in the activities of the Panthers and in their deceptions and who remains a faithful keeper of the progressive flame.

Art and I had grown up on the same block in Sunnyside, Long Island—a neighborhood of Queens that had been colonized by the Communist Party, to which our parents belonged. Because Art was a few years older than I, we were not close as children, but became friends after college when we found ourselves together in Berkeley in the early 1960s as members of the nascent New Left. Art was a "movement" progressive, a day-in-day-out "street" activist in the organizations that made up the antiwar, countercultural left. Even his job was movement related. He was a staff writer for the *Berkeley Barb*, the activists' political organ.

Towards the end of the 1960s, Peter Collier and I were editing *Ramparts*, the most successful and well-heeled journalistic institution of the left. Because Art was an old friend of mine, we took him under our wing and gave him writing jobs that supplemented his income, while Peter devoted considerable time and effort to rewriting Art's pieces to meet the literary standards of a national magazine, more demanding than those of an "underground" paper like the *Berkeley Barb*. I mention this only to establish that no personal animus explains the communication he sent.

From his position at the *Berkeley Barb*, Art made himself particularly serviceable to the Black Panther Party, which he tirelessly promoted as a persecuted vanguard of the progressive cause. His propaganda was so valuable to the Panthers, that eventually he was assigned to write the official biography of Charles Garry, the lawyer who defended Newton from charges that he had murdered a young policeman named John Frey. Newton had indeed committed the murder, but in Art's account, and in all the writings of New Leftists at the time, Newton was presented as the innocent victim of a racist conspiracy by the state. It was writings like Art's that prompted other New Leftists to think of Newton as "one of them," a black leader they could trust.

Art and another friend named Marty Kenner were the New Leftists closest to the Panthers of anyone I knew. Kenner was a successful stockbroker who had organized the famous Leonard Bernstein party that Tom Wolfe satirized in *Radical Chic*, but was working virtually full-time as Huey Newton's personal emissary and financial adviser when I became involved with him. Newton had sent Kenner to various European capitals to appeal to their governments to bar Eldridge Cleaver from entry. Cleaver was living in Algeria, where he had fled to escape the law, and from where he had challenged Newton as a "sell-out" who had betrayed the revolutionary cause.

In the 1960s, I had kept my distance from the Panthers because I was frightened by their gun-toting style and hectoring tone. As the 1970s began, Newton announced that it was "time to put away the gun," and "serve the people." It was this political posture that had caused Cleaver to denounce him. And it was at this juncture that I became involved with him and with the school project I have already mentioned. At first, I had intended just to raise the money for the school, but when Marty Kenner withdrew unexpectedly—telling me only that he was "burned out"—I was left with the task of organizing the school myself, and I recruited Betty Van Patter to keep its books.

As I have already indicated, I had not seen or heard from Art Goldberg or Marty Kenner for fifteen years when I received Art's letter. It seems obvious what provoked his communication. I had just published a book called *Hating Whitey and Other Progressive Causes*, one of whose chapters, "Black Murder, Inc.," is a memoir describing how the Panthers killed Betty. Obviously it was reactions to this publication among his political comrades that prompted his decision to contact me.

What I found most interesting in his letter, in addition to his denial that he is still political, was that though I have written hundreds of pages on the details of Betty's murder, of my involvement with the Panthers, of my own responsibility and guilt for her death, and of the devastating impact it had on me and my family, Art Goldberg seems not to have read any of them.

November 19, 1999

Dear David,

Every so often I hear about something you've written that pisses somebody off, but I don't much care because I have pretty much retired from politics.

One thing I have been meaning to tell you for years, however, concerns the death of Betty Van Patter, the *Ramparts* bookkeeper.

In my mind, you are the person responsible for her death. [Emphasis in original.] Sending her in to audit the Panthers' books at that particular time was tantamount to dressing her in a Ku Klux Klan white sheet and sending her up to 125th Street in Harlem or to West Oakland.

I distinctly remember warning you to be careful about getting too involved with the Panthers because things were getting pretty crazy at the time you jumped in. I had pulled back, Marty Kenner had pulled back and so had Stew Albert.

Had you asked Stew or myself, we would have urged you not to send Betty into the school under the circumstances in which you did. . . . The fact that you let Betty deal with them directly was incredibly naïve on your part, and shows you had no idea of what was going on with the Panthers at that time. If you had asked Stew, myself or Marty, we could have told you . . . . Kenner, after all, knew a lot about the Panther finances, as he was a major fundraiser. Nothing happened to him. . . .

The problem was that you were inexperienced and naïve and Betty Van Patter got killed because of it. That's why, whenever anyone brings up Betty's death, after you've written about it or alluded to it, I always say, "It was really Horowitz' fault. He set her up." As I said, it was like putting her in a white sheet and sending her up to Harlem.

Just wanted to let you know what I've been thinking.

Peace,

Art

Here is my reply:

December 12, 1999

Dear Art,

Unlike you I don't pretend to have "retired from politics," and unlike you I try not to lie to myself. Having become a conservative, I am prepared for how pathetic, vicious and disloyal some human beings can be, and how sublimely unaware of the disgusting image they present to others even as they preen their moral selves for their own approval. As a result, your letter does not really surprise me.

The fact that you should have spent ten seconds carrying around your insipid thoughts about Betty's death is laughable. Nonetheless, I thank you for revealing how ignorant you are about yourself and your friends, and how you are still wallowing in the evil that once engulfed us all.

Marty Kenner as my possible savior. If only I had thought of that! It was Marty, of course, who left the Panther school project in my hands—and without bothering to say why. The same Marty was so far from thinking the thugs he was among were bad guys that ten years later he attended the great Huey P. Newton's funeral as a fan, and then played the role of behind-the-scenes sponsor of Panther Field Marshal David Hilliard's self-glorifying book just before he became president of the Dr. Huey P. Newton Foundation, and resident tour guide of historic Panther sites. Stupid me! Why didn't I think of asking Marty for help?

"Nothing happened" to Marty, as you put it—nobody raped and tortured him and then bashed his head in (as I would phrase the same)—because his nose was so far up Huey's rear end right to the last that he couldn't get his tongue loose to annoy them, even if it had occurred to him to do so.

Give this, at least, to Betty. She wasn't killed because she was white or stupid. She was killed because she had the integrity and the grit to talk back. She wasn't spineless like you and your friends. She was killed because she wasn't a feckless servant of rapists and murderers like you and Marty were then and apparently still are now.

And Stew Albert!!! How could I have overlooked good old Stew when I was in need of advice? Stew Albert, the Yippee genius who wrote a letter to *Ramparts* calling me a police accomplice because in an editorial I had condemned the SLA's assassination of a black father of three children, whose only crime was to have been a superintendent of schools. My editorial gave a "green light" to law enforcement to carry out the richly deserved execution of Stew's beloved SLA fruitcakes! With stand up talent like this, Art, you should really go on Leno.

I see you are still crusading for social justice—going around telling anyone who has read my latest feeble attempt to right this historical record and show the world what we did: "It was really Horowitz' fault. He set her up." Don't worry my friend. I'm not going to return the favor and say you did it and I didn't. Of course, you did write all those rave notices and cover-ups, encouraging others to help feed the Panthers' criminal appetites (or has age affected your memory of this?). But I'm still not going to tell people it was your fault that I got involved with the Panthers or recruited Betty, or even that you kept your mouth shut all the time I was down in Oakland putting my life and hers in danger.

Of course, you've already prepared your alibi. You told me "things were getting pretty crazy at the time." What was I supposed to make of that? "Crazy" could mean that the police were after them, that some of them were "agents" or that these pressures were creating internal conflicts I had to look out for. DID YOU TELL ME THAT HUEY NEWTON WAS A F——— MURDERER AND MIGHT KILL ME?!!! Of course you didn't. In fact, everything you had written or said to me about Huey Newton told me exactly the opposite. And that is all that you've ever written to anyone or said to me about Huey and his progressive gang to this day.

But I still won't point my finger at you now, or blame you for what I did then. I won't do that because that's how I fell into this mess in the first place. By blaming others for what I did or did not do, by blaming them for my own malaise. And that's what your self-serving politics is finally about, Art—yours and Marty's and Stew's. It's about putting responsibility where it doesn't belong. It's about blaming everyone but yourselves. It's about getting others to blame anybody besides themselves for who and what they are.

I'm glad you wrote this letter. It makes all the pain, and all the wounds inflicted on me by you and your comrades since then seem worth it. Because it shows me what wretched human beings I was involved with when I was one of you—a member of the progressive vanguard and at war with the "enemies of the people."

Your letter shows me that in all these years you haven't changed a bit. But I have, and it's the only thing in this whole mess that I'm not sorry about.

By the way, the "Peace" salutation at the end of your letter was a really nice touch.

David

The Nation *at the Millennium*

L OOKING BACKWARDS, the twentieth century was mostly a stage
for the destructive dramas of a secular religious faith called
"socialism." It is a faith inspired by the dream of a social
redemption realized through human power rather than divine,
through politics and the state. In its communist form, this faith
ruined whole continents and destroyed a world of human lives. Have
we learned from the disasters—or will its passions follow us in the
years to come?

For an answer I turn to the pages of the *Nation*, an institution of
the left that participated in these dramas across the entire century,
and whose editorial stances on each defining moment of the communist project have been utterly refuted by historical events. The
editors of the *Nation* supported the Russian Revolution and the
Stalinist collectivization, the infamous purge trials and the Nazi-
Soviet Pact, the Soviet conquest of Eastern Europe and the Maoist
despotism in China, the Communist conquest of South Vietnam
and Pol Pot's genocidal revolution and, of course, Castro's long-lived
tyranny in Cuba.

During the Cold War, the editors of the *Nation* opposed the Truman Doctrine, the formation of NATO and SEATO, and the efforts of western military and intelligence organizations to stem the Soviet tide. Over five decades, the editors of the *Nation* waged journalistic war against the defenders of freedom in the West, against America's "cold warrior" presidents Truman and Kennedy, Nixon and Reagan. At the same time the *Nation* was the chief defender of Kremlin shills and Soviet spies like Harry Dexter White, Owen Lattimore, John Stewart Service, and the Rosenbergs. At the end of the century, its editor-in-chief was still defending Alger Hiss.

The editors of the *Nation* should have been able to hand down to each other whatever lessons they had learned from their errors. But like the Bourbons, they seem to have learned nothing essential and forgotten nothing as well. During the slow unfolding of the marxist collapse, the socialist movement they fostered was often fragmented. But at the beginning of the new millennium the believers of this progressive community of faith are more influential in Amcrican political and cultural life than they have been at any time in the American past. They populate the White House and the Congress; they are the sitting leadership of the AFL-CIO and of the principal academic professional associations that relate to society and the arts, and of many of the most important institutions of the media as well.

In the premillennial hour, the editors of the *Nation* ran two stories—an appraisal of the socialist century past and a harbinger of the socialist century to come—that provide an answer to the question posed above.

A long review article appeared in the December 13, 1999, issue called "Exploiting a Tragedy." It was written by the *Nation*'s longtime "European Editor," Daniel Singer, a godson and disciple of the Trostkyist writer Isaac Deutscher and the magazine's resident expert on the subject of Communism. The main focus of the article was

The Black Book of Communism, a French treatise that attempted to sum up the human horror of the project to make a better world. According to the book's authors, during the twentieth century between eighty-five and one hundred million human beings were slaughtered in peacetime by marxists in the effort to realize their impossible dream. In a foreword to *The Black Book* Martin Malia suggests "any realistic accounting of Communist crime would effectively shut the door on Utopia."

That is the least one might expect to learn from the unbroken record of the socialist utopias of the century just past. But it is exactly the lesson the *Nation* fervently rejects. Writes Singer: "Our aim—let us not be ashamed to say so—is to revive the belief in collective action and in the possibility of radical transformation in our lives." He refers to this passion for social redemption as "the Promethean spirit of humankind," a term that reprises the precise language Marx used when he launched his destructive project over 150 years ago. Socialism is dead; long live socialism.

For Singer and the *Nation,* the unrelieved horrors and failures of socialist experiments over the course of a century are not sobering lessons, not reasons to reconsider the faith. They are just a tragedy of errors that need never be repeated. For the *Nation* it is the story of "a revolution in a backward country failing to spread and the terrible result then presented to the world as a model." In other words, had there been enough Communists in America and Europe to make revolutions there as well, the utopia that socialists dreamed of would have been realized the world over.

In the very next issue the *Nation's* editorial hailed the eruption of political violence to protest a world trade conference in the state of Washington as a beacon of socialist renewal in America.* The

---

* Marc Cooper, "Battle in Seattle," *Nation,* December 20, 1999.

protest by radical environmentalists, anarchists, and trade unionists against the emerging global market was, the *Nation* declared, "something not seen since the Sixties," when the anticapitalist, antimarket, antiproperty forces of the left last took their socialist fantasies and nihilist agendas to American streets. The voices the editorial recorded were all too familiar: "A week ago no one even knew what the World Trade Organization was," proclaimed Tom Hayden, one of the most destructive Luddites of the previous generation, who did not miss the opportunity to join the demonstration. "Now these protests have made WTO a household word. And not a very pretty word."

From generation to generation, the message also had not changed: "A corporate-dominated WTO that puts profits before people and property rights before human rights can no longer sustain its current course," declaimed the editorial. It quoted Gerald McEntee, a leader of government unions and a major power in Democratic Party politics: "We refuse to be marketized." Recycling famous words first uttered by a 1960s radical, McEntee proclaimed: "We have to name the system, and that system is corporate capitalism."* In other words, at the turn of the millennium, the *Nation*'s war was still directed against a system that in the past fifty years had brought unparalleled well-being to billions of people who previously had been excluded from all but the barest minimum of the fruits of their labor from the beginning of time—a system which is the only creator of democratic freedoms the world has ever known.

The *Nation*'s familiar mantra—"Profits before people and property rights before human rights"—was anathema to the system that Marx formulated originally. How was it possible for any sentient

---

*   This is a restatement of Carl Oglesby's famous 1965 presidential address to the Students for a Democratic Society, known as the "Name the System" speech.

human being to have lived through the twentieth century and retain this socialist delusion? How was it possible to witness the tragedies of this epoch without understanding that property rights form the basis of any rights human beings have been able to secure? Or that far from conflicting with human needs, as marxists maintain, profits are the only practical engine ever devised that succeeded in fulfilling them to any reasonable degree?

Such willful ignorance does not stem from lack of intelligence, but has a deeper source in human desires that can only be satisfied by religious faith. The socialist dream of achieving a kingdom of heaven on earth is as old as Eden. "You shall be as God" was the serpent's fatal promise in the Garden. It is the same "Promethean" dream that Marx claimed as his own and that the *Nation* editors intend to keep alive. It is the idea of redeeming the world through human action, of putting a human design on the impersonal structures of social order beginning, of course, with the economic market. In wishing for this outcome, socialists fail to understand that markets which human beings cannot control, like an edifice of law that they must obey, are disciplines that we require in order to be human.

Without such restraints and the limits of such restraints—as all history attests—humanity will quickly descend into the very barbarism that twentieth-century events have made so familiar and whose lessons—as we go forward to the twenty-first—the *Nation* and its comrades have still to learn.

13

A Cup Half Full

ONE OF THE PRINCIPAL SOURCES OF HUMAN MISERY is a tendency that exists in all of us to take for granted what we are given and to fail to appreciate what we have. There is even a folk wisdom that makes us aware of this, reminding us to be wary of those who see the half-empty glass when the tumbler is half full. From the most intimate relations that take place within families to the political battles that determine the fate of nations, this simple error in perspective has been the cause of incalculable human suffering from the beginning of time.

In our century alone, visionaries of the left, who rejected the order they inherited, took part in the murder of a hundred million human beings in pursuit of an impossible socialist dream. In the name of "social justice" and in order to "make a better world," leftists destroyed the political and economic structures of whole societies that had evolved organically in the course of time. What they actually produced for their efforts, however, was not something better than what had been, but worse: a suffering greater than the world had ever seen.

When the Communists seized power in 1917, Russia possessed a democratic parliament. Its agricultural economy was able to produce a grain surplus that was exported to countries abroad. But Lenin's revolutionaries viewed Russia's fragile capitalism as a cup half empty compared to what they imagined a socialist regime could accomplish. Consequently, they did not think twice about decapitating Russian democracy and destroying its agricultural order. They would create a future that was better than both. Freed of the restraint of custom and law, the liberators went on to slaughter forty million "enemies of the people" (mostly peasants) and put tens of millions of others in concentration camps. All this was necessary, they said, to build a "worker's paradise." But they were able to build no paradise. Instead they produced a world of famine, poverty, and economic ruin.

In a message to high school students at the beginning of the millennium, the film director Oliver Stone reprised these destructive passions of the left, disparaging the freedom America had given him and millions of others in favor of the familiar socialist dream.* "Essentially our freedom, our democracy, is a consumer freedom," Stone told them. "What refrigerator do you want, what television do you want, what car do you want, is it Fab or Ajax?" This challenge was typical of the irresponsible reflex of intellectuals like Stone who dismiss the fruits of capitalism as though they were nothing. As though the enormous privileges of wealth and freedom bestowed by this system had simply fallen on them and all of us like manna from heaven.

But the reality is quite different. With the exception of a miniscule few privileged individuals, for most of recorded history almost all the inhabitants of all societies spent their entire waking hours work-

---

* Stone's message and the author's reply appear in *Fast Times*, March 2000.

ing at hard physical labor just to keep from starving or to be warm enough to stay alive. For millennia the pursuit of the arts, literature, and the sciences, the ability to spend a great portion of one's life pursuing what one pleased, were treasures available only to royalty and aristocratic elites. Today, as a result of the capitalist market, even the poor among us have amenities—running water, flush toilets, refrigeration, modern medicine, central heating, motorized transport, telephones, radio, television—that were unavailable to the richest people just one hundred years ago. Today, the power available to virtually every American citizen in the form of an ordinary personal computer is greater than the power wielded by any factory owner in the nineteenth century. On an ordinary personal computer—available to virtually every man, woman and child, thanks to the power of the market—one can produce a newspaper or a film, reach tens and even hundreds of millions of individuals and access uncensored information that was unavailable even to kings in previous ages.

To Oliver Stone and leftists like him, this is nothing. It is less than nothing. It is an inspiration for outrage. Because of this cornucopia of "consumer" wealth, democracy itself is a sham. Dismissing nearly a thousand years of struggle in behalf of popular sovereignty and democratic choice, Stone admonishes his high school audience thus: "Instead of wasting a lot of time reading about Tweedledum and Tweedledee for President, ask yourself. . . : Who owns America?. . . . Who owns the media? Where does the money go?" To Oliver Stone and leftists like him "these are the key questions" on the threshold of the millennium: "This is what is controlling your 21st Century future."

Nonsense. The answer to these questions is readily available, and it is the opposite of what they are meant to insinuate. *You* own

America. We do. Literally. Today, half of America owns shares in American companies and within decades virtually every American citizen will be a capital owner too. Stone himself is a self-made multi-millionaire, paid handsomely by capitalists to slander and abuse them—the very corporate oligarchs he pretends to fear. But Stone cannot accept the freedom corporate America gives him. (Instead, he is the very epitome of bitterness and paranoia. It grates on him that others have more than he does.)

But if Bill Gates does have one hundred billion dollars, what of it? Gates's money is invested in companies that create jobs and provide services for millions of customers all over the world. Nor is he free to lord it over them as Stone's fantasy suggests. The rule of the market is as strict as it is liberating. If the companies in which Bill Gates invests do not serve and satisfy their customers, others will. In doing so they will drive their competitors out of business. Even with one hundred billion dollars Bill Gates is no Sun King but must serve his customers. Additionally, he must obey the government they elect, which can punish his company if it abuses its power—and already has.

Like hormonal adolescents, left-wing social critics like Oliver Stone overflow with resentment and spiteful rage. They are mad because they weren't smart enough to make one hundred billion dollars, and they want others to be mad too. They blame (and want you to blame) "corporate capitalists"—the very creators of this incredible universe of human services, products, and opportunities. They want you to make the creative and successful avatars of the business world pay for whatever individual frustrations you feel. And they do not want anybody to say otherwise. Leftists will ferociously attack "bad people" who disagree with them about the benefits of capitalism, while claiming to be persecuted themselves. They will attack those who have succeeded in our free society, attempting to infuse such attacks with historical romance:

> So you have a choice I think [writes Stone]—it's a tough choice because those of you who are students may not know the world very well yet, but the more you know it the more you find your-self hostage to these forces, corporate and state forces that seek to control your mind and your inalienable right to the pursuit of your own conscience. You have that decision to make in your lifetime, . . . that decision is whether you're going to live like a slave or whether you're going to live like Spartacus, the famous Roman gladiator slave who led a revolt against his masters—and fight for your freedom and deny the bastards their victory over your soul.

This is the message to high school students, in America, on the threshold of the millennium! Leftists like Stone appeal to human weakness, to the roiling resentments, irresponsible angers and feelings of powerlessness that each of us harbors. "What am I really feeling as opposed to what I think I should be feeling . . ." is the guide that Stone proposes to his high school readers.

My advice is this: Feelings, whether authentic or false, are often the worst guide to what is real. The feeling that one is persecuted by Jews or threatened by homosexuals or blacks is what drives the haters among us. The feeling that capitalists and corporations control people and exploit them and stifle their freedom is the force that inspired Communists to kill millions and lay waste to nations.

Instead of feelings, let knowledge be the guide, particularly historical awareness of the human past. History is the record of our human experience and, more important, our human limits. History teaches a powerful lesson: Better to work with the world we have and improve it step by step, than to seek a revolution that will wipe out the past and everything we have so painfully learned.

14

Roads Not Taken

A STRANGER SENT AN E-MAIL TO MY WEBSITE a while back that posed two questions I had been thinking about for some time, and seemed therefore uncannily personal. "I was curious," the correspondent said, "if you have ever looked at your political 'apostasy' and wondered whether, if circumstances had been different—if you had not been involved with the Panthers or if your friend had not been murdered by them—you would still be a Marxist today. Was your apostasy a result of an inexorable intellectual development, or were you forced into your second thoughts?"

In some form or another, it is a question that everyone gets around to asking himself. *If circumstances had been different, if I had made this choice or avoided that one, would my life have been different?* If the answer is yes, which are the circumstances that would have made me different? It is a question as old as philosophy—the mystery of free will.

Not everyone, of course, experiences such a dramatic turning in his life as I did when the Black Panthers murdered my friend, Betty Van Patter, twenty-five years ago. But we all have them. Roads taken and not taken. Decisions that changed our lives, and perhaps ourselves as well. Such changes can be personal as well as intellectual, but each time they occur we face the question once again: Are they essential to our being? Or are they only secondary to who and what we are?

In my own case, I find it easier to answer when the question is about my intellectual development. I do not know that the intensity of my ideological transformation and the tone of my politics would have been different if they had not been provoked by an act of brute criminality committed by my political allies. But I am confident that the change would have come. I have many friends and acquaintances who had "second thoughts" similar to mine, in which they found themselves rejecting the ideas and understandings that motivated them when they were young. I have no reason to suppose it would have been different for me.

In fact, one of the first pieces I wrote about the episode that changed my political life was an article called "Why I Am No Longer A Leftist" that appeared in 1986 in *The Village Voice*. It drew explicit parallels between the crime the Panthers had committed and the much larger and more famous crimes for which the left itself was responsible that had caused others like me to reconsider their beliefs. As a leftist I had developed habits of mind that caused me to look at "classes" rather than individuals, at social structures and paradigms rather than events and personalities, particularly if they could be viewed as incidental or unique. (Many leftists have written to dismiss my change with the remark "Why should one mistake matter?", suggesting that what the Panthers did was aberrant to the radical experience rather than typical.) This same attitude, which I once shared with the left, made it important for me to analyze my own mugging by reality to decide whether it was a characteristic and not merely contingent event before I could allow its lessons to affect my outlook as a whole. In the article I wrote for *The Village Voice*, as later in my memoir, *Radical Son*, I did just that.

The personal question is not so easy to resolve. Why do we move in the grooves we do? Why are there such ingrained patterns to our lives? Patterns like these were evident my directions then, as they are now. But nobody who knew me then and now has failed to note the difference. I wouldn't want to exaggerate the changes that have occurred, but they have. The trauma of this murder and of the betrayals that followed profoundly affected me, changing me from what I once was, or otherwise might have been.

If you ask, I will tell you that it was the pain that did it. Pain is the spur that gets us to move. Every day following Betty's murder the pain hammered my heart, and broke down my resistance. It said to me: *You cannot stay in this place. If you do, you will die.* It is fear that restrains us and keeps us in our familiar grooves. But when I was caught between fear and pain, pain proved to be the greater force. It was pain that overcame the inertia. It was the need to escape a death of the spirit that caused me to alter my course.

My correspondent's second question was an unexpected one, more perplexing than the first: "Do you ever feel that you are wasting your breath? Do you think that truth will ever matter? No matter what you prove or disprove, in the end the truth will remain in the shadows of what people want to hear and want to believe."

I agree more than I care to with this thought. It is the human wish to be told lies that keeps us as primitive as we are. On the other hand, such stoic realism is, after all, what being conservative is about. It is about accepting the limits that are absolute that life places on human hope.

One could define the left as just the opposite: the obstinate, compulsive, destructive belief in the fantasy of change — in the desperate hope of an earthly redemption. I have watched my friends whose ideas created an empire of inhumanity survive the catastrophe of their schemes and go on to unexpected triumph in the ashes of their defeat. Forced to witness the collapse of everything they once had dreamed and worked to achieve, they have emerged unchastened by their illusions searching for a renewal of their faith. The society they declared war on has even rewarded them for their misdeeds. Today they are cultural navigators in the land most responsible for their worldwide defeat. I cannot explain this dystopian paradox except by agreeing that politics is indeed irrational and socialism, a wish as deep as any religious faith. I do not know that the truth must necessarily remain in the shadows. But I am persuaded that a lie grounded in human desire is too powerful for reason to kill.

Index

Beckett, Thomas, 148
Bennett, Bill, 68, 74–77
Bentley, Elizabeth, 135
Bergman, Lowell, 171
Berkeley, 162
Berkeley Barb, 173
Berlin Wall, xiii, 57
Berman, Paul, 141
Berns, Walter, 77
Bernstein, Helen, 51, 52
Bernstein, Leonard, 173
bilingualism, 28
Bill of Rights, xi, 74, 77
Bizreit University, 156
The Black Book of Communism, 180–81
Black Caucus, 22
Black Entertainment Television, 98, 151
Black Panther Party, 164, 190
  Goldberg and, 173–78
  killings of, 170–72
  support for, 170
  Van Patter's death and, 169–70
black separatism, 100–103, 118, 146
Blumenthal, Sidney, 14, 22, 126
Boehlert, Sherwood, 68
Bok, Derek, 92
Bonior, David, 26
The Book of Laughter and Forgetting (Kundera), 72
Bork, Robert, 77, 141
Bortin, Josephine, 162
Bortin, Michael, 162–63
Bowen, William, 92
Boxer, Barbara, 12, 21, 22
Bradley, Bill, 108, 117, 120–21, 146
Bradley Foundation, 118
Brady Bill, 139
Brahms, Johannes, 148
Brawley, Tawana, 108

Brown, Elaine, 169–70
Brown, Jerry, 169
Brown, Ron, 40
Buber, Martin, 156–57
Buckley, William F., 135, 141
Bureau of Justice Statistics, 87
Burns, Gary, 86
Bush, George, xiv, 40-44, 86
Bush, Jeb, 40

California, 34, 170
  1998 elections in, 26–29
  Kuehl's election in, 44–46
  "three-strikes law" and, 36
California Civil Rights Initiative, 46
Canada, 28, 71
capitalism, xii, 118, 187
Carlson, Margaret, 96
Carnegie, Andrew, 118
Carter, Jimmy, 74
Carter, Stephen, 143
Carville, James, 14, 22
Castro, Fidel, 179
censorship, 65–72
Chambers, Whittaker, 132
Charen, Peggy, 69
Chekhov, Anton, 147–48
Cheney, Lynne, 74
Chen Han-shen, 133
Chenoweth, Helen, 68
Chicago Seven, 164
China, 6, 35, 57, 130, 179
Chomsky, Noam, 119–20
Christian Coalition, 13, 67
Christian Right, 21, 67
Churchill, Winston, 123
Civil Rights Act, 37
civil rights movement, 83–84
  contemporary, 108–12
  defense of criminals and, 86–88

A Note on the Author

David Horowitz is the author of such best-selling books as *Hating Whitey* and *Radical Son* and, with Peter Collier, co-author of *Destructive Generation*. A leader of the New Left in the 1960s, he grew disillusioned with the consequences of radicalism in America and abroad, and by the 1980s his political about-face was complete. Mr. Horowitz lives in Los Angeles, where he is president of the Center for the Study of Popular Culture and editor of the journal *Heterodoxy*.

This book was designed and set into type
by Mitchell S. Muncy,
with cover art by Stephen J. Ott,
and printed and bound
by Thomson-Shore, Inc.,
Dexter, Michigan.

The text face is Caslon,
designed by Carol Twombly,
based on faces cut by William Caslon, London, in the 1730s
and issued in digital form by Adobe Systems,
Mountain View, California, in 1989.

The index is by IndExpert,
Fort Worth, Texas.

The paper is acid-free and is of archival quality.

25